THE ADVENTURE TRAVELER'S HANDBOOK

How to safely explore the world in bold new ways

Nellie Huang

The Adventure Traveler's Handbook: How to safely explore the world in bold new ways

© Copyright 2013 by Nellie Huang

All rights reserved. No part of this publication may be reproduced, stored in or introduced into a retrieval system, or transmitted in any form or by any means (electronic, mechanical, photocopying, recording or otherwise), without the prior written permission of both the copyright owner(s) and the above publisher of the book.

Library and Archives Canada Cataloguing in Publication

Huang, Nellie, 1982-, author
    The adventure traveler's handbook : how to safely explore the world in bold new ways / Nellie Huang.

ISBN 978-1-927557-06-8

    1. Adventure travel--Guidebooks. 2. Outdoor recreation--Guidebooks. I. Title.

G516.H82 2013   910.2'02   C2013-905171-6
                                                                                  C2013-905172-4

Disclaimer:

This book provides entertaining and informative snapshots of the author's personal experiences while exploring the world, as well as stories and anecdotes from other travelers. The Adventure Traveler's Handbook is not meant to serve as an exclusive checklist to effectively safeguard the reader in every travel situation, and is sold with the understanding that neither the author nor the publisher intend to render any type of medical, legal, or professional advice. No one can guarantee safety and travel can expose everyone to potential risks. Because safety is impacted by each person's actions and choices, each reader assumes all responsibilities and obligations with respect to any decisions made as a result of the use of any content in this book. While all reasonable measures have been taken to ensure the quality, reliability, and accuracy of the information in The Adventure Traveler's Handbook, author and publisher make no warranties or guarantees, expressed or implied, by providing content in this book. Any implied warranties of merchantability or fitness of use for a particular purpose are also disclaimed. Neither the author or publisher, nor any contributor, will be liable for damages arising out of or in connection with the use of The Adventure Traveler's Handbook. Because of the dynamic nature of online media, certain web addresses or links contained in this book may have changed since publication and may no longer be valid.

*To every single traveler I've met along the way,
thank you for inspiring me.*

Acknowledgements

I have so many people to thank for helping shape this book into what it is.

First of all, my heartfelt gratitude goes to Janice Waugh, the creative brain behind The Traveler's Handbook series. Your patient guidance and thoughtful feedback helped me to get from the starting point to the finishing line, and for that, I am eternally grateful. Special thanks to Candace Rose Rardon for your sharp editorial eyes, professional advice, and unfaltering support in all of my projects. Thank you for inspiring me in so many ways.

I am also grateful to friends who have helped improve the numerous drafts of this book: Lola Akinmade, Jeff Jung, Jodi Ettenberg, Shannon O'Donnell, and Sarah and Terry Lee. To Steve Keenan, Dave Cornthwaite, and Trent Holden, thank you for taking the time to read and review my book. It is an honor to have your help. Many thanks also to Alastair Humphreys, Alex Cowan, Jeremy Albelda, Kenza Moller, Rebecca Enright, Molly Blaisdell, Iain Mallory, Debra Corbeil and Dave Bouskill for sharing your stories and thoughts in this book. More gratitude goes to my editor, Tracey Nesbitt, and book designer, Ana Botelho.

Grateful thanks to my husband Alberto for supporting me every step of the way and sharing all the ups and downs of long-term travel with me. I'm also indebted to my father, who pushed me to take that first leap and showed me how to live life fearlessly. To my mother and sister, thank you for having faith in me.

Lastly, a sincere thanks to all the readers of WildJunket.com, whose support has kept me going and striving for more. I would not be who I am today without you. This book is for you. Thank you.

Table of Contents

The Backstory: Stumbling Upon Adventure 1

Seeking an Extraordinary Life 5
What Makes an Adventure? 6
Who Is This Handbook For? 8

Laying the Groundwork 13
Tackling the Basics: Where to Go 17
Timing It Right: When to Go 18
Going Independently or With a Tour Company 20
Choosing a Tour Operator that Suits You 23
Trip Ideas: Themed Adventure Tours 25
    Expedition Cruises 25
    Wildlife Safaris 26
    Trekking Trips 26
    Volunteering Trips 26
    Overland Journeys 26

Pre-Trip Planning 29
Budgeting For Your Trip 34
Saving Before You Go 35
Technical Planning for Outdoor Sports 38
    Trekking 38
    Cycling 40
    Scuba Diving 41
    Kayaking or Canoeing 45
    Skiing or Snowboarding 46
Technical Gear List 52
How to Find a Pack that Matches Your Needs 56
What to Look For in Outdoor Clothing and Footwear 57
Packing Suggestions 62
Physical and Mental Training 66
Protecting Your Health 72
Building a Safety Net with Activity and Travel Insurance 77

Table of Contents

On the Road **79**
    Overcoming Your Fear 83
    The Dangers and Rewards of Traveling to Forbidden Lands 86
    Risk Management in the Outdoors 93
    Staying Healthy While Traveling 103
    Responsible Travel Ethics 107
    Handling Setbacks: What to Do When Something Goes Wrong 113

An Adventure Awaits **116**

Resources **117**

Endnotes **124**

Reference Boxes
    15 Best Destinations for Outdoor Adventures 27
    How to Find Unique Experiences and Get Free Accommodation 36
    A Step-by-Step Guide to Packing 65
    Tips to Prevent Acute Mountain Sickness 75
    Managing Your Fear in 5 Steps 85
    Winter Survival: How to Avoid an Avalanche 102
    How to Keep Fit While on the Go 106

Travel Stories
    Burma's Open Arms 10
    Learning Life Lessons from Sharks 14
    Biking for a Cause 21
    Cycling a Continent 30
    In the Face of Unpredictability 49
    On the Top of the World at Everest Base Camp 69
    Where Fear Meets Faith: Finding Courage in Life 80
    Seeing Past the Headlines in North Korea 89
    When Tourism Goes Wrong 109

The Backstory: Stumbling Upon Adventure

I was 14 when I did my first bungee jump. But it was hardly of my own will.

My father was the one who always wanted me to be brave and fearless. I remember traveling to Indonesia, Australia, and elsewhere with my parents when I was young, and my father was the one who pushed me to try new experiences and soak it all in like a sponge.

I was shy, timid, and spoiled by creature comforts and urban living in the metropolis of Singapore. Camping out in the wild or hiking for days was out of the question. I was cocooned in my own ignorant bliss, and my dad was determined to change that.

There I was, 165 feet above the tree canopy in the middle of tropical Thailand, legs wobbling and heart pounding like a loud drum roll. I shouted out to my guide, "I can't do this! There is no way I'm jumping!"

But it was too late to back out. He gave me a hard push on my back, and within seconds I was free falling through the humid, wet air, head first towards the ground. My hands were flailing in all directions while my lungs screamed. Blood rushed to my head, which by now was spinning like a top.

All of a sudden, a strange thing happened: I felt a bolt of electrifying energy surge through my body. My fear was replaced by a refreshing wave of adrenaline. I was cheering and clapping by the time I reached land, and I wanted to do it all over again.

I've been hooked ever since.

That rush of energy was what first sparked me to try out new things, and to approach life with an open mind. I held on to it and it became a huge part of who I am. I knew then that I did not want a normal life.

Nellie Huang

After graduating university with an engineering degree, I packed my bags and left to see the world with my husband, Alberto. Adventure became a theme that linked our travels. From our base in London, we went on weekend hikes in Greece, road trips around Turkey, and cultural immersions in Morocco to savor delicious cuisine and get lost in the souks.

These short jaunts eventually evolved into longer and deeper experiences: we spent a few months volunteering in Tanzania, backpacking through Latin America from the southern tip of Argentina all the way to Guatemala, and zigzagging across Southeast Asia on a three-wheeled tuk-tuk.

By the time we left London, I had turned my curiosity about the world into a quest for adventure. I have since trekked through the stone forests of Madagascar in search of lemurs, kayaked in the backwaters of Alaska, skydived in Spain's Costa Brava, and swum in the sub-zero waters of Antarctica. My life now revolves around adventure travel, and I spend almost nine months of each year on the road, seeking out fresh new experiences.

I often look back at the old me and imagine how life would be had I not taken that jump. I might not be who I am today. That leap pushed me to steer away from conformity and fight off monotony. I have faced numerous obstacles that have come my way, and have developed more self-confidence and independence as a result. In this book, I hope to show this is possible for you too.

I encourage you to seek out your own adventure. We all make our own stories, so why not make yours a hell of a good one?

One of my favorite travel experiences: skydiving in Costa Brava, Spain.

SEEKING AN EXTRAORDINARY LIFE

"We all have the extraordinary coded within us, waiting to be released."
Jean Houston

What Makes an Adventure?

Adventure travel has been around for more than two centuries, tracing its roots back to explorers such as Edmund Hillary, who completed the first successful ascent of Mount Everest, and David Livingstone, the first European to see Victoria Falls. They truly revolutionized the way we see the world.

Today, modern travelers continue to push beyond the boundaries of commercial tourism. In the broad sense of the word, adventure travel in our modern world is less about discovering new places and more about exploring the world in inspiring and exciting ways.

Adventure has evolved to become a loose term. It can be about challenging yourself to your physical limits or broadening your knowledge of far-flung places, people, and cultures. It can also mean bringing help to people in need through volunteering or other humanitarian work. It can even simply mean trying something for the first time.

To put things into perspective, an adventure doesn't have to involve climbing mountains or biking across continents. A gap year in Southeast Asia can be an adventure for a first-time traveler, while visiting under-the-radar Iran is quite an undertaking even for the hardened traveler.

Ultimately, adventure is a state of mind more than anything else. It is about having the inspiration to conquer something you once thought unreachable. It is about believing in yourself and having the faith to achieve something you want. Whether you succeed or not, it doesn't matter because the act of pursuing adventure doesn't set you back — it only pushes you forward.

In this book, I will be sharing lessons I have learned from more than a decade of travel. I have also invited several other writers, expedition leaders, and long-term travelers to share their knowledge and shed some light on how adventure travel has molded their lives. I urge you to find out what adventure travel means to you by asking yourself these questions:

- What do you want to gain from your adventure — more knowledge, self-confidence, first-hand experiences?
- How do you want to challenge yourself – to step out of your comfort zone or simply try something for the first time?
- Which are the most important aspects of adventure travel to you — physical obstacles, deep cultural immersions, or far-flung destinations?

> *We all have our own frontiers to push, be it an expert spelunker venturing into a newly discovered cave system or a toddler dipping his toes in the Pacific for the first time. Adventure travel is also an enormously powerful tool. Done in the right way it can bring knowledge, empathy, wealth, and peace to people and places.*
>
> Daniel Raven-Ellison
> National Geographic's geographer

Who Is This Handbook For?

Readers of my travel blog, WildJunket, as well as friends and family, have often expressed concern about the way I travel, and interest in doing it themselves. More often than not, I have found that most of them want to be more adventurous. What's stopping them is self-doubt.

"I wish I could do it, but I don't think I'm brave enough," is a remark I've heard too often. The fact is, everyone has fears – including full-time adventurers and professional sportsmen – but it all boils down to how we manage our fear and turn it into something positive.

In line with my travel blog and magazine, WildJunket, this book is created with the hope of inspiring readers to conquer their fears with the right mix of motivation, preparation, and safety precautions.

Over the following chapters, I have compiled my personal tips and combined them with inspirational stories to provide basic tools for aspiring travelers to venture out on their own. For active travelers, I have also added sections that zoom in on five popular outdoor sports: trekking, cycling, scuba diving, kayaking/canoeing, and skiing/snowboarding.

Whether you are a first-time adventurer or a seasoned traveler looking for something different, I hope this book will encourage you to take a step into the world of adventure.

Embracing adventure at Glen Helen Gorge in Australia's Northern Territory.

Burma's Open Arms

The enormous bell rang overhead, thousands of candles flickered, and the smell of incense filled the air. Row upon row of monks, dressed in swaths of burgundy cloth, sat praying with heads bowed and knees bent. Hundreds of young ladies gathered in the impressive Shwedagon Paya, brooms in hand, ready to sweep out all the bad luck of the past year and welcome a new beginning.

I had arrived in Burma (renamed 'Myanmar' by the government in 1989) on a very auspicious date – the Burmese New Year or Thingyan, the most celebrated festival in the country.

After years of isolation, Burma is finally welcoming tourists again. Since a new civilian government replaced the military junta in November 2010, political reforms have taken place. The military released Aung San Suu Kyi from house arrest, and her political party, the National League of Democracy, lifted the boycott on tourism in 2011.

During my visit, election signs were everywhere – symbols of the new era. For decades, military rule had deprived citizens of basic democratic rights such as freedom of expression and even the right to vote. Now, things seemed to be looking up.

The Burmese were hopeful about their future, as I discovered while chatting with a local taxi driver. "Things are finally changing in Burma," he said, with a sparkle in his eyes. "We've waited for so long."

For now, Burma is still on the road to recovery. An air of dusty nostalgia hangs around every corner, locomotives run on engines from the 1960's, and people ride on run-down trucks and water-buffalo carriages. Men saunter along wearing the traditional longyi wrapped around their waists, their mouths blood red from chewing on betel nut; women's faces are painted with thanaka, a white, natural sun protector made from tree bark.

Traveling here is an adventure: there are few ATMs, little Internet access, no cell phone reception, and a refreshing lack of global brands and hotel chains. For first-time travelers, it can be overwhelming, but once you've adjusted to the old-world atmosphere, Burma's charm is irresistible.

Back in Shwedagon Paya, the festive mood was growing, and people's spirits were rising. The 'Golden Pagoda', poised on a hilltop in the heart of the city, is the most revered religious site in the country, and many locals were checking in to the temple for several days of praying and volunteer work during the festive season. The temple ground was buzzing with life as people streamed in with offerings and prayers for the year ahead.

Navigating into the city center, I found the streets clogged with locals splashing one another with buckets of scented water. On the boulevards, teenagers grooved to Burmese pop music blasting through the amplifiers. Pails of water rained down on us like a monsoon as we basked in echoes of laughter, cheers, and well wishes. It was the best introduction to the country I could possibly have wished for.

Celebrating Thingyan at the beautiful Shwedagon Paya temple in Yangon, Burma.

LAYING THE GROUNDWORK

"The journey of a thousand miles begins with a single step."
Lao Tzu

Learning Life Lessons from Sharks

In the far distance came a spray of water and the faint outline of a shark's dorsal fin above the gleaming surface of the water.

Zipping over the choppy waves on a chilly autumn morning, we were making our way towards the shark-infested open sea. Gaansbai, in the Western Cape of South Africa, is home to one of the world's densest populations of great white shark.

As we inched close to the animal, the great white revealed itself: its sharp teeth piercing above the water's surface, its fin slicing through it like a knife, and tiny round eyes skillfully scouting us out as we stared in amazement.

Earlier that morning, our resident marine biologist, Matt, had given us a crash course on the great white shark. I had qualms about diving with sharks at first: Is it safe? Are they feeding the sharks? Most of all, is this ethical?

Thankfully, Matt cleared all the doubts in my mind. While movies have made the great whites appear to be mindless killing machines, they are not as lethal as one would imagine. Research finds that great whites, who are naturally curious, do not prey on humans; rather, they are sample biting to discern if the object is food. They will usually not attack unless provoked. Matt used an amusing analogy to explain our risk factor: statistically, we are more likely to get killed by a falling coconut than a shark.

Sadly, the great whites are an endangered species due to overfishing and collisions with shipping vessels. Poachers and ships kill more than 100 million sharks of all kinds worldwide each year.[1] There are only about 3,500 white sharks left in the ocean today. A shortage of sharks could be disastrous to the health of the ocean and its food chain.

The tour operator we traveled with was deeply involved with various research and conservation projects to help save the shark population, and conserve the ecosystem in the area — organizing shark diving trips was only a part of it. To ensure that people do not disturb the sharks' natural habitat, they protect them from being harassed, abused, or fed.

Back on the boat, I zipped up my wetsuit and entered the sturdy steel cage that would be lowered into the choppy, cold water. As I dipped my snorkel mask beneath the surface, I immediately caught a glimpse of the enormous shark. The animal was swinging its torpedo-shaped body and blade-like tail from side to side. The look in its eyes was haunting, and it seemed to be looking straight at me. Suddenly, the shark headed straight for our cage, and almost crashed against the iron bars that separated him from us.

I dove straight up through the water's surface to catch a breath of air, overwhelmed by the close encounter. The sounds of my palpitating heart and rapid breathing echoed through my ear drums.

One shark after another appeared before our group of divers, circling our cage from the front, back, and even bottom. The smell of the fish oil was pungent, and the rough seawater was choking me with each breath I took, but the sharks were too distracting. I spent the morning observing their behavior. It was difficult to associate such seemingly ferocious creatures with what I had learned about them earlier, but it definitely gave me a glimpse into the sharks' world.

That day, my impression of the great whites was forever changed. What I got out of the experience was not just a tick on my bucket list, but rather the opportunity to learn the truth about the great white sharks through an intimate, first-hand encounter. The truth can be very different from what we have been taught or choose to believe. And only by experiencing places, animals, and human interactions for ourselves do we learn what actually lies beneath the surface.

Swimming with sharks in Gaansbai, South Africa, changed my impression of the great whites forever.

Tackling the Basics: Where to Go

The first step is to ask yourself a set of questions to determine what you want to get out of this experience. If you're looking to fulfill specific goals or enjoy a particular sport, this gives you a great starting point to make your decisions.

Does a specific type of activity interest you? Are you an experienced scuba diver or cyclist looking to find a suitable place to pursue your hobby? If you are keen on diving, consider going for a live-aboard boat trip in Thailand as a budget option or a cruise that mixes up diving and cultural visits in Fiji. For those interested in multiple-day hiking, the Camino de Santiago in Spain or Peru's Inca Trail can be great ways to experience the countries' back roads. Setting a goal for yourself defines a structure for your trip.

Are you looking for soft or extreme adventures? Do you prefer 15 days of non-stop trekking at high altitudes or are you more comfortable with a one-week trip of rafting and light hiking in Costa Rica? Are you looking for a tough challenge or simply seeking an exciting way to see a new country? In either case, I would advise spacing out your schedule with a mixture of adventure and relaxation to ensure you have enough downtime to kick back and enjoy the surroundings.

Is comfort a key factor for you? While some travelers enjoy camping in the wild, other adventure seekers may not want to compromise on comfort. In either case, there is always an option to suit you. Expedition cruises are a great way to explore less-visited corners of the world onboard luxury vessels. Wildlife buffs can also stay in luxury tented camps, and have the opportunity to sleep in the wild without sacrificing comfort.

What are your levels of experience and skill? Consider your fitness level and try to match it with a trip that fits your interest. Those who are experienced in a particular sport, but haven't yet tried it abroad, should familiarize themselves with the safety regulations in their destination and research the reliability of the tour operator.

> *"Every day at work is an adventure, as unpredictable weather and shifting sea ice force us to constantly reassess our options as we explore the islands of Svalbard, the great northern ice pack or the tumbling glaciers of Antarctica. I've worked amongst polar bears, orca, blue whales and king penguins in the pursuit of new places and a better understanding of some of the coldest and most remote places on Earth.*
>
> *Adventure travel is more than just an active holiday - it can take you to places you never expected."*
>
> Alex Cowan
> Geologist and expedition leader

Timing It Right: When to Go

For adventure travelers, the best time to travel often depends on what activity you'll be engaging in. Seasonal sports such as ice-climbing or canyoning can only be done during a particular time of the year.

Are you planning on white water rafting in the Grand Canyon? Check when the rivers flow at their highest. Want to trek Mount Kilimanjaro? Read up to learn which time of the year has the best weather conditions. Regardless of where you want to go and what you plan to do, getting the time right can vastly enhance your experience.

Keep these factors in mind when deciding when to travel:

- Check the best time to visit your desired destination using Best Time to Go (BestTimetoGo.com), destination blogs, and guidebooks.
- If you only have a certain time period to travel, find out if the main activity you want to do will be affected. Will your chances of seeing wildlife be affected? Will you still be able to go paragliding? How is the weather during that time of the year?
- Are you going on a career break or a short one-week trip? Either way, deciding on the length of your trip gives you leeway to plan your budget.

If time is not an issue, I recommend visiting during the shoulder season for your destination. You'll find the best value for money, without the crowds. While shoulder season often means lower chances of, let's say, seeing a polar bear or the northern lights, you'll probably be compensated by milder climate and more affordable prices. To find out when the shoulder season is for a destination or particular activity, check with your travel agent to determine the period when tours run less frequently and prices are not at their highest.

Canyoning can only be done during certain time of the year when there is enough water to do leaps — Bled, Slovenia.

Going Independently or With a Tour Company

For the adventure traveler, going with a tour company can provide you with safety and technical guidance. In fact, many sports, such as scuba diving or rock climbing, should not be practiced alone. However, traveling independently gives you plenty of flexibility and freedom that guided companies cannot offer. Weigh the pros and cons to decide which style suits you best.

Pros and Cons of Organized Travel

Pros:
- Takes care of all details including activities, lodging, and transportation.
- Reduces stress of travel by providing you with a pre-arranged itinerary.
- Packs in as many activities as possible for time-crunched travelers.
- Ensures safety in numbers and provides companionship.
- Reduces your expenses, as activity costs and taxi fares can be split with group mates.
- Allows you to reach remote places that are difficult to access as an independent traveler.
- Provides emotional support and camaraderie when faced with physical challenges such as long treks.

Cons:
- You will have to follow the group and may not be able to explore on your own.
- You need to compromise with travel mates when it comes to making decisions.
- You have less chance of meeting other people and locals.
- You may have to endure traveling with people whose company you don't enjoy.
- You may need to pay a single supplement if traveling alone.
- You don't necessarily save money by traveling with a tour company, as some don't cover all expenses.

Biking for a Cause

"Welcome to our home," said Vivian, our guide for the bike tour. Vivian grew up here in Masiphumelele, a township at the edge of Kommetjie in the Cape Peninsula of South Africa. Like the other 45,000 people living in the township, her parents and grandparents had moved here in the 1980s to find work and a better standard of living.

Today, about forty percent of the people here are unemployed, and most live in less than favorable conditions. Shelter and air circulation are inadequate, fire is a constant threat, the sewage disposal system is dysfunctional, and HIV is a major concern.

The area was named Masiphumelele, meaning "we will succeed" in Xhosa, in hopes of a brighter future.

Beaming with energy, Vivian welcomed our group of travelers into her community as we hopped on our bikes to take a tour around town. At first, I struggled with the manual back-pedal brakes on my old-style Dutch bike, but I soon found myself whizzing through the dusty back streets of Masiphumelele, waving to locals along the way.

"On bikes, you get closer to your surroundings. You have many more opportunities to interact with the community than you would have from a tour bus," said Sally Peterson, the director of the bike tour company, AWOL Tours.

It was Sally's love for cycling, combined with her compassionate attitude towards the community, which sparked the idea of a bicycle township tour. Sally was a finalist in OutThere Magazine's 'Adventurer of the Year' award in 2001 after cycling from London to Cape Town to raise funds for Survival International.

Back on the bikes, it was time for lunch and we stopped for a short break at Kwa Nongolooza's Place, a simple and cozy shack that resembled a makeshift street-side kiosk. The smell of barbequed meat seeped through the corrugated tin roof. There was no cutlery, just our hands; so we ate like the locals.

I dipped my fingers into the pale white pap (maize porridge commonly eaten all over Africa), and kneaded it into dough, before drenching it with rose-red chakalaka vegetable relish. I mixed it all up with some off-the-grill pork chops and sausage, and happily licked the sauce off my fingers. By this point, I had tried plenty of local foods, but this simple lunch turned out to be my favorite meal in Cape Town.

After we had filled our stomachs, we continued to pedal past more tin-roofed shacks, one right next to another, alongside severely polluted water canals and dusty alleys. On the other side of the road, however, were a few newly erected apartment buildings. Vivian told us this new housing was built by the government to support the growing population of Masiphumelele. Aid was coming in to the township, albeit slowly.

We then made a stop at the Masiphumelele Library, a center where people came to study, use the communal computers, and develop careers. Funding for the library comes from a coalition of local organizations, volunteer teachers and tutors. Here, we met several young children, who quickly befriended us. One of the girls held my hands as we toured the library, and even hopped on my bike to join us on the ride.

As we bid farewell to our new friends, we left with an unspoken joy, happy to have had a chance to take a peek at the locals' lives and contribute just a little to this community.

Getting to know the community in Masiphumelele made a difference to our experience in Cape Town, South Africa.

Choosing the Tour Operator that Suits You

Outdoor activities are never 100% safe. Take extra precautions and do your due diligence when researching the reliability of an adventure tour outfitter. Check the reputation of the company and its accident history by reading reviews on blogs and talking to past clients via Twitter or Facebook.

Make sure the company's values are consistent with your own. In my case, I look for companies with an eco-conscious policy and a responsible tourism strategy. I also prefer operators that emphasize cultural authenticity and contributing to ocal communities.

A good starting point is adventure.travel a consumer website from the Adventure Travel Trade Association (ATTA). You can find tour operators sorted by activity or destination expertise, and read traveler reviews and trip listings.

Here are some questions to ask when picking a company to travel with:

- How experienced are the guides? It takes years of experience to become an expert. A professional guide or instructor who is comfortable and confident in his or her element will put you at ease.
- What is the student to instructor or guide ratio? This depends on what activity you're doing. One-on-one is often mandatory for high-risk sports, although the ideal number for diving is three or four students/divers per instructor.
- What type of equipment is provided? Is it well maintained? Are there any backup systems in place? This will determine how professional the company is.
- Is the operator affiliated with the country's official association (e.g. United States Parachute Association) or does it have any international accreditation?
- What is included in the prices and what will cost extra? Check if meals and transfers will be provided.
- What is the cancellation and rescheduling policy? Many extreme sports are subject to weather and other unpredictable conditions; make sure you will be refunded in case of cancellation.
- What types of people usually travel with this company? You don't want to be diving with people you cannot trust, or traveling on an overland truck for a month with travelers whose company you do not enjoy.

Trip Ideas: Themed Adventure Tours

In today's competitive market, the array of adventure trips offered by tour operators is boundless. These are some of the most popular and interesting choices.

Expedition Cruises

Featuring small-scale vessels, expedition cruising has a strong focus on responsible, educational and meaningful travel. These cruises usually include adventure-oriented activities, Zodiac-boat excursions, and informative lectures conducted by experienced biologists, geologists, or naturalists. They take guests to far-flung and less accessible regions such as the Arctic, the Antarctic Peninsula, and Alaska's Inside Passage, for a first-hand experience in some of the world's most fragile environments.

Zodiac boat excursions allow close wildlife encounters while expedition cruising in Antarctica.

Wildlife Safaris

Wildlife safaris are high on many people's bucket lists for the rare opportunity to get up close and personal with animals in the wild. Wildlife watching often involves camping and touring around in a jeep, although walking safaris and canoe safaris are also popular. People looking for more comfort will be pleased to know there are luxury-tented camps in many remote parts of Africa. Tanzania's Serengeti National Park and South Africa's Kruger National Park are excellent places to see the Big Five (lion, elephant, buffalo, leopard, and rhinoceros), while Uganda's Bwindi Forest is great for seeing gorillas in the wild.

Trekking Trips

Put your endurance to the test and scale mountains of epic proportions on multi-day trekking trips. Not only do they bring out the best in you both physically and mentally, they also give you an opportunity to visit areas that are otherwise difficult to access. The Holy Grail for trekkers remains the highest mountain in the world, Mount Everest, standing at 29,029 feet above sea level. For a more attainable goal, most people head to Mount Everest Base Camp, which is still an arduous twelve-day trek from Lukla, Nepal.

Volunteering Trips

Working with communities is a great way to see the world and give your services to worthy causes at the same time. Whether your skill lies in teaching, medical services, or manual labor, there are always projects that need a willing hand (even an untrained one). For time-crunched travelers, many tour operators offer short-term volunteering trips in Cambodia, Laos, and Peru that combine tourism with community-based experiences. Refer to 'The Volunteer Traveler's Handbook' for more detailed information.

Overland Journeys

With rising awareness of environmental conservation, many people are now avoiding the use of planes and ships and turning to overland travel, a more eco-friendly and flexible option that allows the experience of traveling the back roads of a country. Overland trips organized by tour operators usually involve traveling in multi-purpose trucks that pack in cooking facilities and camping tents, and have seating capacity for 10 to 30 passengers. They are also often cheaper and more time-efficient than independent travel.

15 Best Destinations for Outdoor Adventures

I have compiled a list of some of the most recommended places for each outdoor sport based on research and tips from experts.

Mountaineering or Trekking
- Annapurna Circuit, Nepal — one of the most popular and picturesque treks in the Himalayas.
- K2's base camp, Pakistan — the crown jewel for hard-core trekkers, which requires a certain level of physical fitness to accomplish.
- Inca Trail, Peru — an ancient trail that leads from the Sacred Valley to Machu Picchu, through ruins and terraced slopes.

Cycling
- Pacific Coast Highway, USA — a spectacular coastal road that follows Highways 1 and 101 from Oregon to Los Angeles.
- Carretera Austral, Chile — a partially unpaved road that weaves through Patagonia's lakes, mountains, and glaciers.
- Karakoran Highway, Pakistan — a classic route between China and Pakistan that takes you across the highest paved border in the world.

Scuba Diving
- The Great Barrier Reef, Australia — the world's largest reef with an amazing diversity of marine life.
- The Galapagos Islands, Ecuador — a group of remote islands that are home to unique marine animals such as penguins, sea lions, and hammerhead sharks.
- Palau, Micronesia — an island of unique geology, home to healthy populations of hawksbill turtles and manta rays.

Kayaking or Canoeing
- Phang Nga Bay, Thailand — paddle among limestone karst columns, remote caves, and pristine coves.
- Glacier Bay, Alaska — weave through the fjords and lakes that crisscross this national park.
- Baja California, Mexico — glide alongside seals or California gray whales in the Sea of Cortez.

Skiing or Snowboarding
- Whistler and Blackcomb, Canada — two side-by-side mountains with more than 200 marked runs, 16 alpine bowls, and three glaciers.
- Aspen, Colorado — world-famous mountains for skiers of all abilities, as well as free riding terrain on the backside.
- Chamonix Mont Blanc, France — located at the foot of the highest peak in the Alps, with one of the world's longest ski runs.

Macchu Picchu, the final destination for trekkers on the Inca Trail.

PRE-TRIP PLANNING

"A goal without a plan is just a wish."
Antoine de Sainte-Exupéry

Cycling a Continent

Dave Bouskill and Debra Corbeil, publishers of The Planet D (theplanetd.com), have conquered many challenges, from climbing Mount Kilimanjaro to camping in Antarctica. Here, they share the experience that prompted them to become full-time adventurers.

It all started with a glass of wine on a rainy New Year's Eve. We had come home early from visiting family in Florida and felt that it was time for another adventure. We didn't want to just simply go backpacking again. We wanted to do something extraordinary.

As we discussed how unfulfilled we were with our lives, an interview on the CBC, Canada's national public broadcaster, caught our attention. The interviewer was talking with ultra marathon runner Ray Zahab, the original inspiration for the wildest adventure of our life. Ray Zahab had competed in and won many ultra-marathons such as the Marathon des Sables and the Yukon Ultra, featured in the 2007 documentary 'Running the Sahara'.

By the time we went to bed, our minds were made up and we decided that by the next New Year's Eve we were going to be on the adventure of a lifetime. Two weeks later, we spotted an article in the paper about a man who was taking part in that year's Tour d'Afrique. It is an insane bicycle race that starts in Cairo, Egypt and ends in Cape Town, South Africa.

That was it. We immediately joined a spinning gym and started our training for the world's longest and most grueling cycling race. We informed our friends, families, and our employers that we were leaving and, before we knew it, the time had come.

One year later, we were on a plane to Egypt. We had been cycling an average of 250 miles per week, and had been weight- and endurance training all year. But nothing could prepare us for the physical challenges that lay ahead. We would be traveling through some of the toughest terrain on the planet, cycling, on average, 75 miles per day for 120 days.

It was a cold morning in January when we left in a pack from the Great Pyramids of Giza. Sixty people from twenty-three countries had come together to ride through a continent. Half of Cairo's police force was out to escort us through the city. They stopped traffic and people cheered as we passed. We felt like major celebrities in our convoy as we worked our way through the maze of this enormous urban center.

It was surreal at times, to say the least. In Egypt and Sudan, we had armed guards following us through our route. Random trucks would pull up in front of us with their machine guns aimed in our direction. They would smile and wave, and we would hold our breath and pray their hand wouldn't slip or their truck wouldn't hit a bump.

Each day brought on a new challenge and adventure. In Egypt, we had to dodge speeding buses and hectic traffic. In Sudan, we dealt with deep desert sand and unbearable heat. Tanzania and Malawi brought on epic climbs and awesome descents. We survived being chased by wild packs of dogs and even baboons. We were lost in the desert and rode with herds of cattle and donkeys. But nothing compared to having children throw rocks at our heads during our entire twenty-three days in Ethiopia.

As time went on, things became easier. The roads got better the farther south we cycled. We camped our way down the continent, meeting new people and seeing awe-inspiring sights such as Victoria Falls, Mount Kilimanjaro, and Fish River Canyon. We slept under the stars surrounded by nothing except nature, and we lived a life of simplicity for four months. As grueling and difficult as it was, there was something beautiful about waking up each day and knowing exactly what you had to do.

Cycling Africa pushed us to our physical and mental limits, and after conquering 7,500 miles on the seat of a bicycle we have learned that anything is possible.

Riding into Cape Town on our final day in May brought a sense of pride and personal achievement. A huge crowd greeted us, and we were even rewarded for our efforts. I won the women's race and Dave was awarded the prestigious EFI (Every Fabulous Inch) award. While others went on side trips or took a day off, Dave had pushed through sickness and fatigue to ride every single kilometer of the tour.

Our time in Africa had come to an end, but a spark had been lit inside us. This was only the beginning, and a whole new world of possibilities had opened up.

Debra Corbeil and Dave Bouskill cycling the back roads of Ethiopia during the Tour d'Afrique race.

Budgeting For Your Trip

Whether you are a novice or an expert, keep in mind that you can travel the world without breaking the bank. Plan your budget based on your values and priorities. Here are four steps to take when setting your budget.

1. **Identify your big-ticket items.**
   These are the items that take up a big portion of your budget. Airfare is usually the first thing you need to pay for when planning a trip. Other major expenses include activities and travel gear.

2. **Estimate your expenses for accommodation, meals, and transportation.**
   Check Lonely Planet guidebooks and wikitravel.org to find the approximate cost of meals and accommodation in your destination. To get an estimate of transportation costs, learn how to get from one city to another, how long it will take, and how much each leg will cost.

3. **Don't forget to include expenditures on visas, travel insurance and vaccinations.** Even if you are planning a one-week trip, you should still purchase travel insurance. Check the last half of this chapter for more information on these items and their costs. If you are planning to buy specialized technical gear, be sure to estimate the cost of these equipment in your budget.

4. **Identify your priorities.**
   Would you rather spend money on scuba diving or on a four-star hotel room? Do you want to eat meals at a fancy restaurant or enjoy street food? Would you prefer to go on a three-day trek into the mountains, or splurge on a helicopter ride? Deciding what your priorities are will help you decide how you want to spend your money.

5. **Start planning your trip early.**
   You will want to enjoy the excitement of the planning process, rather than the panic of not having sorted out your travel arrangements.

Saving Before You Go

Be it a week's trip in the Rockies or a year-long jaunt around the world, we all need to save our pennies in order to go on an adventure of a lifetime. Here are some tips to help you reach your financial goal:

- Create a spreadsheet, and start tracking every item you purchase or every payment you make. Do this for about a month to get an idea of where your money is spent. You can then consciously decide how you need to change your spending habits.
- Try budgeting and expense tracking tools like Mint and PearBudget that will suggest ways to cut your expenses and help you count down towards your goal.
- Do some research to find a high-interest savings account. Many banks offer free checking and savings accounts without monthly fees.
- Prioritize your expenses and give up unnecessary items. Use the library for books and DVDs. The next time you want to buy something, ask yourself if you really need it. When you do need to buy certain items, try to buy them used.
- Go through your closet, garage, and storage to find items you no longer use. Have a garage sale or sell them online at Amazon, eBay or craigslist. Selling your unwanted things can boost your savings dramatically.
- Change your lifestyle by cooking at home more often. Invite friends over instead of eating at restaurants. Visit places that offer free admission, such as museums or art galleries.

How to Find Unique Experiences and Get Free Accommodation

Student backpacker and journalist Kenza Moller shares ways to save money and gain interesting experiences at the same time.

Couchsurfing
Couchsurfing allows you to find couches to crash on during your travels and provides the option of hosting travelers at your place.

Couchsurfing lets you verify members' identities using a credit card, and read reviews from their previous surfing or hosting experiences. Similar sites include Global Freeloaders, Servas, and the Hospitality Club.

House-sitting
Want to stay in a house abroad rent-free? If you are willing to water the plants, do some cleaning, and feed the pets, you may just be the perfect house-sitter for someone. Trusted House Sitters has a big range of house-sitting gigs on offer around the world, as do HouseCarers and The Caretaker Gazette.

Work for accommodation
WWOOFing (World Wide Opportunities on Organic Farms) has grown in popularity as a method of traveling. Organic farms around the world provide travelers with accommodation and food in exchange for volunteer work on the farm. Similar working programs can be found at GrowFood, Help Exchange, and Workaway – and not all of them are related to farming.

Become a deckhand
If you love the ocean and traveling, there are several websites that provide a place for boaters and travelers to connect. Hard work is expected of you, but you will get a roof over your head and the opportunity to sail to several different locations. Listings can be found at Work Boat, Crew Bay, and All Yacht Jobs.

Volunteering in Tanzania not only gave me a chance to save money on lodging and explore the country slowly, it also taught me plenty of life lessons.

Technical Planning for Outdoor Sports

An adventure-themed trip often involves one form of outdoor activity or another, whether that means backpacking in Europe or scuba diving around the Pacific. These activities tend to involve more detailed technical planning than other pursuits. Keep in mind that the type of planning depends on your own priorities and preferences, regardless of what activity you choose to do.

Trekking

Whether you are an independent trekker or you intend to travel with an operator, be sure to check with your doctor whether the expedition suits your fitness level and experience. In the physical training section, I also advise travelers to go for a mountaineering consultation at an altitude center before attempting the trek.

For independent trekkers, consider the terrain, weather, and the experience of your group when planning how many miles you will travel each day. Experienced hikers in good shape can usually do ten to 25 miles per day, depending on terrain, while novices should plan on six to 12 miles. Don't be overambitious – aim for less, rather than more, so you can take time to enjoy yourself.

Check to see if your destination requires permits or other advance preparation. For instance, all trekkers in Nepal require a TIMS (Trekkers Information Management System) card before a trek. Camping also often requires a permit, available for a small fee payable in cash only.

It is advisable to bring your own technical gear for trekking to ensure it meets your particular needs. It is simply not worth skimping on quality boots or using makeshift walking sticks. If you have made the effort to travel halfway around the world, don't allow your ambitions to be destroyed by the wrong gear.

Useful resources for trekking enthusiasts:

- **Mountain Zone** (mountainzone.com) provides technical tips on using GPS devices and camping stoves, preventing high-altitude sickness, and more.
- **Summit Post** (summitpost.org) is a community-based site with information on routes and trip reports. Articles are mainly centered on American routes.
- **Trailblazer Publications** has a series of trekking guide books covering destinations from the Dolomites to the Himalayas.

Hiking in the extreme heat of Australia's King Canyon can be challenging even for hardened travelers.

Apps:

- **AllTrails** (free) is a maps application that shows accurate distances, and trailheads all around the world.
- **MotionX GPS** ($1.99) provides real-time voice navigation, and a searchable database of locations.
- **Elevation Pro** ($0.99) gives your exact location using Google Maps, and compares USGS altitude with your GPS.
- **Woodall's RV & Camping Copilot** (free) lists the RV park or campsite closest to your location (only in North America), using your phone's GPS.

Cycling

I am a terrible cyclist, but I have gathered the help of some experts to help you plan your cycling tour.

Most travelers who have cycled around the world say experience is helpful, although by no means required. Karl Creelman, the first Canadian to ride around the world, only learned to ride a bicycle a few weeks before making his decision to circle the globe in 1899.

Friedel and Andrew, publishers of Travelling Two (TravellingTwo.com), cycled more than 37,000 miles, through 30 countries, during a three-year cycling tour. They, too, started bike touring with almost no cycling experience, but ultimately decided to try bicycle touring as they wanted to travel independently and experience places in between. The tips below are excerpted from Travelling Two with their approval.

> For those who are planning their first bike tour, start by plotting your route and determine how much distance you can cover on your bicycle tour. Start with a distance close to 40 miles a day if you're new to bike touring, or even 25 miles if you're traveling with young children, or on a route that is particularly mountainous. Remember to leave room for rest days, bad weather and sightseeing along the way.

Useful links:

- **Adventure Cycling Association** (adventurecycling.org) offers inspirational stories and practical resources, including a network of 41,420 cycling routes around the world.
- **Bicycle Touring Pro** (bicycletouringpro) is a blog written by Darren Alff, and includes specific budgeting tips, packing for a long-term biking trip, and destination-focused biking advice.
- **Travelling Two** (travellingtwo.com) is a global biking blog that includes country-by-country biking notes, and a breakdown of expenses, as well as packing lists and technical tips.

Apps:

- **Strava** (free) tracks all your rides, allowing you to analyze your performance in detail, and compare your speed and time with local riders.
- **Cyclemeter** ($4.99) is another ride-tracking app that measures your heartbeat and condenses it into a graph or table.
- **Garmin Fit** ($0.99) is a training app that links up with fitness sensors to track your performance.
- **Bike Doctor** ($4.99 on iOS, $2.99 on Android) is a popular bike repair app that comes with step-by-step guides for common problems.
- **Coach My Ride** ($2.99) provides structured training and workouts for time-crunched beginners and professionals.

Scuba Diving

It is important to keep in mind your experience level when planning a scuba-diving trip. Divers should research their desired locations to find out what conditions they are likely to encounter, and whether any special skills are required. Beginner divers will be more comfortable doing shallow dives with a sandy bottom, while night and wreck dives are more suitable for experienced divers.

If you are learning to scuba dive, I recommend diving with PADI (Professional Association of Diving Instructors), as it is the most recognized certification in the diving arena. Try to choose a dive center with a minimum of a PADI five-star rating (based on certification programs, gear selection, and scuba experience). The PADI Basic Open Water certification process usually takes three or four days, and consists of classroom lessons, an online test, pool sessions, and open-water dives. You can choose to complete the classroom and pool sessions at home, and your dives at your destination. Alternatively, you can do the whole process at your destination, although that takes up more of your vacation time.

If you are planning a trip centered on diving, you might like to consider a live-aboard dive cruise, where you'll be diving daily from the comfort of a small-scale vessel. These live-aboard packages usually include a certain number of dives each day, cabin accommodation, food, weights, and weight belts, as well as the guidance of a professional dive master.

Remember to wait at least twenty-four hours between diving and flying. Higher altitude means lower outside pressure, and this means that residual nitrogen in the diver's blood can emerge as bubbles if the ascent isn't slow enough.

Dive master Charli Moore, who writes about her diving adventures around the world on Wanderlusters.co.uk, shares her tips:

> When planning a dive trip, consider the climate, tides, and predicted weather patterns at the destination, and try to visit when conditions are optimum.
>
> If you do not already have a policy, buy dive insurance and talk to the insurers about emergency evacuation coverage offered at your destination. I also always find out my proximity to a decompression chamber, just in case.

Useful links:

- **PADI** (padi.com) has a website with a list of accredited dive shops, technical know-how on dive gear, as well as a larger community. With its free app, you can download your PADI eCard, which is an electronic version of your PADI license.
- **Diveboard** (diveboard.com) maps out dive sites and shops around the world recommended by divers. It also allows you to connect and communicate with fellow divers.
- **Plan Your Dive Trip** (planyourdivetrip.co.uk) lists a range of dive sites, clubs, and operators in the UK, as well as recommended books on diving in the area.

Apps:

- **Dive Log** ($12) allows you to keep an electronic record of your dives, and transfer data from certain dive computers to your electronic device.
- **Diving Dude** (free) has similar features, together with a number of social networking functions.
- **Nitrox Calculator** (free) gives you an easy way to calculate the right blend of enriched air for nitrox divers.
- **Scuba Exam** (restricted version is free; full version is $4) is great to brush up on your dive theory, or to quiz yourself before you take the exam.
- **Marine Tides Planner** (free) is great for independent divers; it has a long list of global ports and delivers tide predictions with clear charts and numerical tables.

Scuba diving in the Galapagos Islands surrounded by a tornado of cardinal fish.

Kayaking or Canoeing

A kayaking trip or expedition can be quite a challenge to plan if you are going independently and without experience. Do as much research as you can on the various factors impacting your journey, including weather, logistics, topography, the conditions you're likely to encounter, and your skill level. Determine whether the location has the right kind of features for your trip. Is there enough water to paddle at that time of year? Are there convenient landings with good approaches and sheltered coves?

For a novice kayaker, determine your paddling capacity before you set out, perhaps by testing yourself on a weekend trip. I recommend setting daily distances by reducing the maximum distance you can paddle by half. For example, if you can usually handle fifteen miles per day, plan to paddle seven to ten miles per day. If you bite off more than you can chew, you'll feel pressured to over-exert yourself just to keep on schedule. It's also extremely important to be flexible and plan for contingencies.

Useful links:

- **Canoe & Kayak** (canoekayak.com) is a magazine on canoeing, kayaking, and whitewater rafting. It is available in both print and digital formats.
- **Paddling** (paddling.net) has a large community of paddlers, as well as outfitters that organize kayaking expeditions and international rafting trips.
- **Top Kayaker** (topkayaker.net) has a great collection of articles on safety, launch sites, and kayak touring tips.

Apps:

- **RiverGuide** ($4.99) gives you access to thousands of real-time stream flow gauges in the US, as well as kayaking news.
- **ACK Kayak Launch Points** (free) uses the GPS on your mobile phone to identify launch points for your kayak or canoe near your location.

- **Tide Graph** ($1.99) shows tidal details on a graph, as well as the speed at which they are rising or falling.
- **Kayaking GPS** ($1.99) allows you to mark and map out features, and identify your location using the GPS on your phone.

Skiing or Snowboarding

As with the other sports, the most important thing to remember when planning a ski trip is to only choose slopes that fit your skills and experience level. You can find out if a ski resort is suitable for you by checking the vertical drop of the resort (distance between the summit and base of a mountain, measured straight down) on its website.

For those who want to learn how to ski or snowboard, group classes and private lessons can usually be booked together as a package along with your hotel stay and ski pass. By reading reviews on blogs and community sites, choose a resort with easily accessible beginner slopes, i.e. gentle and wide slopes without skiers and boarders racing through them. There should be some slightly harder and longer slopes to progress on to during the week. Also look for user-friendly lifts (gondolas and detachable chairs that virtually stop to allow you to get off).

Ski clinics are great ways to pick up the skill through intensive, week-long classes. These clinics tend to be limited to small groups to give the instructor time to consider each student's technique. Diagnosis of where people are going wrong can include the smallest detail, such as the adjustment of skis and boots.

For backcountry skiers and free riders, make sure you are well prepared with a safety plan, and that your family and friends are aware of your location. Keep yourself up to date with knowledge on avalanche dynamics and safety. Continuous self-assessment is essential to ensure minimal risk.

Useful links:

- **World Snowboard Guide** (worldsnowboardguide.com) includes best places to ride and sleep, covering 1,000 resorts in 63 countries.
- **Snow Rental** (snowrental.co.uk) allows you to book your gear before you go. The equipment is rated by fellow skiers, allowing you to see at a glance which is the best rental shop.
- **Wild Snow** (wildsnow.com) is a comprehensive skiing blog run by Louis Dawson, a specialist in Colorado skiing. His site includes details on avalanche safety and ski descent techniques, as well as reviews.

Apps:

- **Ski and Snow Report** (free) uses your GPS to inform you of snow conditions at resorts near you.
- **Ski Tracks** ($0.99) uses your GPS to not only map where you ski, but also calculate your speed, slope angle, and vertical drop.
- **Ullr's Mobile Avalanche Safety Tools** app ($9.99) works like an interactive field notebook that helps you measure slope angles, create pit profiles, and test for signs of instability.
- **SnoWhere** ($9.99) acts as an avalanche beacon backup, using GPS to turn your phone into a beacon that other SnoWhere users can track.

Skiing in the Swiss Alps can be great fun with the right amount of planning.

> "*I cycled round the world because it was cheap, needed no skill, and I had loads of time available. If I had been rich, and short of time, I might have motorbiked round the world instead. That low skill, low budget, low tech, low administration journey is still the greatest trip I have ever done and has opened every door in my life since.*"
>
> Alastair Humphreys
> National Geographic Adventurer of the Year 2012;
> alastairhumphreys.com

In the Face of Unpredictability

In the midst of the howling wind and falling ice, the bleak display at the top of the Eyjafjallajökull Volcano looked like a scene from a disaster movie. I could barely open my eyes as icy frost whipped across my face. We only had a few hundred feet left to reach the peak, but we were now stuck in a snow storm.

It was the thrill of such unpredictable circumstances that brought my husband Alberto and I here in the first place. The Eyjafjallajökull Volcano's ferocious eruption had made headline news all over the world the previous year, as it spewed hundreds of tons of ash into Iceland's skies and severely affected European air travel. The whole world had watched as explosions of molten lava and ice flashed across televisions.

Families living in the area were evacuated, and layer upon layer of ash descended on Iceland for weeks. Life here was back to normal now and travelers were returning to witness the power of the Eyjafjallajökull Volcano. Although it could erupt again with no warning, we were drawn to this powerful beast of a mountain.

Before we began the trek, we had packed the best possible gear, studied the chances of an eruption, and informed ourselves of the potential dangers. We also made a quick stop at the Eyjafjallajökull Visitor Centre to comb through its artifacts and exhibits to learn about the terrain and seismic conditions. Our guide made sure we knew how to react in case of an emergency. Armed with a positive attitude, we were determined to conquer the beast. It seemed as though nothing could stop us.

That morning the sun made a rare appearance in Iceland's otherwise gloomy autumn skies, casting a shiny shade of gold on the dark green tundra that carpeted the volcano's base. The landscape surrounding us was magnificent: trickling waterfalls cascaded over emerald green moss while the Arctic waters lapped against black volcanic sand on the distant coastline.

As we ascended further, the greenery slowly faded to unveil layers of gray ash spewed from the volcano just a year ago. Glaciers lay beneath our feet, but instead of revealing aqua-blue ice, they were blanketed in solidified lava. It certainly felt we were making a journey to the center of the Earth.

We were just about an hour's trek away from the crater, when things took a 180-degree turn. Thick clusters of clouds loomed high above our heads, and the sunshine was soon replaced by thick fog and heavy rain. All psyched up to achieve our goal, we weren't about to let the weather stop us. We zipped up our water-resistant coats, and continued our trek up the rock-strewn terrain through the extreme cold.

Eventually, large hailstones fell from the sky while heavy snow and a forceful wind whipped our faces. There came a point when we had to take shelter behind a massive tuff rock. We had a difficult decision to make: should we continue up the volcano or turn back before we found ourselves in serious danger? We had come a long way, and it seemed an enormous setback to give up now. However, despite our eagerness to reach the volcano's crater, safety was our priority.

After debating for quite a while in the midst of the snowstorm, our guide made a firm decision: "I think we should respect nature."

He was right. There was little we could do in this inhospitable climate. Even though we never made it to the top of the volcano, we left with a lesson learned: no matter how much you plan, Mother Nature can be unpredictable. After all, she's in charge.

In the snowstorm, we headed down Iceland's Eyjafjallajökull Volcano to stay safe.

Technical Gear List

Most diving, kayaking, camping, and trekking equipment can be hired in areas where these activities are popular. However, if you are serious about pursuing any of these sports, consider bringing your own equipment. When you purchase new gear, try it out before traveling to make sure it works and that you know how to use it.

Most airlines charge an additional fee for bulky gear. Check with your airline as rates vary. It is advisable to bubble wrap your bicycle, surf board, or other gear to protect it. In the case of a bicycle, you'll be required to box it up and deflate the tires. Most bicycle shops can box the bike for a small fee.

The gear recommendations below are aimed for those who pursue these sports on a regular basis. General travel items are found in the 'Packing' section.

Trekking

- Trekking poles
- Safety whistle
- Binoculars
- GPS
- Small daypack
- Water bottle

Camping

- Tent
- Sleeping bag
- Sleeping pad
- Stove and fuel
- Fire starter and matches or lighter
- Cooking and eating utensils
- Water purifier (such as SteriPEN) or tablets
- Garbage bags

Cycling

- Bicycle
- Helmet
- Spare tubes
- Patch kit
- Bike lock
- Racks with panniers
- Bike tools (pedal wrench, spoke wrench, and sockets)
- Pump
- Cycling shorts and jerseys
- Cycling shoes
- Water bottle

Scuba Diving

- BCD (Buoyancy Compensator Device)
- Regulators
- Booties
- Dive computer
- Wetsuit
- Fins and mask
- Pressure and depth gauges
- Mesh bag

Kayaking or Canoeing

- Paddle
- Bilge pump
- Emergency float line
- Emergency signaling devices
- Waterproof bag or case
- Neoprene shirt or wetsuit
- Booties

Skiing or Snowboarding

- Skis and poles or snowboard
- Ski boots
- Goggles
- Helmet
- Waterproof gloves or mittens
- Ski socks
- Insulated and waterproof ski pants and jacket
- Avalanche beacon (for free riders)

Skiers all geared up in Zermatt, Switzerland.

> "I love every facet of snowboarding. It is partly athletic, partly social, and partly meditative. Being outdoors and active in the frigid mountain air is soul cleansing. Sending yourself flying off a forty-foot cliff and landing softly on a forty-degree powder-laden slope is a physical sensation matched by nothing else. Sharing such experiences creates a unique bond among athletes. Paradoxically, when you're moving in long fluid arcs down a mountainside at 60 miles per hour and the only sounds in your ears are the rushing of wind and crunching of snow, you are incredibly alone, lost in a soothing mixture of concentration and mindlessness."

Matt Gibson
Award-winning outdoors and adventure blogger;
matt-gibson.org

How to Find a Pack that Matches Your Needs

When packing for a trip, the first decision to make is the type of luggage you will be using. Consider the type of activities that you plan to do, the length of your trip, and your priorities.

These are the criteria to consider when choosing your pack:

Design: Do you prefer a top loader or a panel-loading pack that allows easy access? A top loader is suitable for long distance hikes as it has a frame structure perfect for comfortable carrying, but not for everyday travel. A panel-loading pack is ideal for uncomplicated packing, but does not provide the best carrying comfort. These days, you can easily find hybrid designs that combine the best features of the two types.

Capacity: It is advisable to keep your pack as small as possible to make loading and unloading a breeze. You need to have a good idea of what you will be bringing on the trip, to determine which pack size you need. Most travelers find that a 60-liter pack is enough to travel for three months or more as it has enough space for the essential items without being too heavy.

Durability: Look for durable material like nylon, and double stitching at weight-bearing points. These features mean your pack can endure rugged terrain and a heavy load.

Carrying comfort: Good packs should be amply padded at the shoulders and hips, and lightly padded on the back. An ergonomic hip belt is great for ensuring comfort as it carries the bulk of the weight.

Fitting: A backpack may fit differently on different people; if you're short, a backpack that is too tall can affect your balance. Most backpacks have gender-specific models. Always try on the pack before purchasing it. If you plan to buy it online, join discussions in travelers' forums to get an idea if it would fit you.

Versatility: Compartments and extra features make it easy to access items. A bottom section is ideal for storing your sleeping sack or hiking boots, while loops can carry a tent or walking sticks. Front and side pockets are great for regularly used items such as a water bottle and flashlight. My personal favorite feature is a zip-off daypack that can be detached and carried separately for a lighter load.

What to Look For in Outdoor Clothing and Footwear

Day Packs
As with all the other items, your daypack only needs to be as technical as the activity you are doing. If your trip centers on scuba diving, it is wise to pick a waterproof pack to keep your belongings dry, while a cycling trip warrants a sling bag for easy access and padded storage.

For most hiking and multisport daypacks, the ideal size is 30 liters. That is enough capacity to hold the essentials and some extra items that you will need for a day. Again, it varies according to intended use: trail runners may prefer to pack as little as ten liters while climbers may need 40 to 50 liters for their equipment.

Here is a quick overview of the different types of day packs and what to look for in each of them:

- **Day hiking packs:** should contain hydration systems and have compartments for loose gear, and side pockets for trekking poles.
- **Climbing packs:** have a narrow profile for rough terrain and features such as ice-axe loops and crampon patches.
- **Ski packs:** should be equipped with a sternum strap, hip belt, and straps to attach skis.
- **Lumbar packs:** have a snug, stable design that is less inclined to shift while running.
- **Cycling messenger or courier bags:** can be worn over one shoulder for easy access and have padded protection for storing electronics.

- **Dry packs:** made of reliable waterproof material, feature welded seams, and have high resistance to UV light and wet conditions.

Clothing

It's said there is no such thing as bad weather, just bad clothing. Whether you are gearing up to conquer peaks, or camp in the savanna, here are some qualities that high-quality outdoor apparel should have:

- **Light, breathable material** – 100% polyester is the lightest and best material for hiking. Avoid cotton, as it is a poor insulator when wet. It makes you feel colder than you actually are, and increases the risk of hypothermia.

- **Moisture wicking** – This diverts perspiration from your skin to the shirt, which allows fast drying.

- **A tight fit:** Purchase a close-fitting shirt to promote moisture wicking efficiency.

- **UV Protection:** Hiking at high altitudes means you are closer to the sun, so you need a shirt that provides adequate protection from ultraviolet (UV) rays.

- **Water-resistance:** When doing water sports, go for clothing with a Durable Water Repellent (DWR) coating for better water resistance. Neoprene shirts and wetsuits also keep you warm while snorkeling, surfing, and diving without restricting your movement.

- **Versatility:** Convertible pants that zip off into shorts or roll into capris provide more clothing options without adding more volume.

Technical Jacket

Today's technical jacket is a product of decades of innovation and creative technologies. It will keep you comfortable and snug even in the worst conditions. To decide which type of jacket best suits your needs, here are factors you should consider:

- Precipitation — is there going to be rain, snow, or sleet?
- Your level of exertion — what type of trekking or physical activity will you be doing?
- Your weight and packing requirements — how light and small do you want it to be?

Types of technical jackets in the market:
- Hard-shell jackets are made using a tightly woven face fabric that is either laminated to a waterproof/breathable membrane such as Gore-Tex® or eVent®, or sprayed with a waterproof coating. They provide protection from wind, snow, and rain, and are lighter and easier to pack than soft-shell jackets.
- Soft-shell jackets are made of stretchable fabrics and are more breathable, even though most of them are not waterproof. They are ideal for dry and cold climates, and winter sports such as skiing.

Insulated jackets feature several warm layers of fleece lining, down, or synthetic filling. Some of them have a hard-shell outer face and are more expensive, while others come with removable inner layers. Personally, I always use a Gore-Tex® hard-shell jacket so I can choose the level of insulation I want, given the conditions, by layering over a fleece or a down sweater. My hard-shell jacket has protected me in extreme conditions from cruising in Antarctica to trekking in Bolivia.

Hiking Boots
Hiking boots not only make walking a breeze, they also provide support and comfort for your feet and ankles on challenging terrain. Luckily for us, they don't need to be expensive to be trail-worthy. There are three general types of hiking boots:

- Low-cut hiking shoes that resemble low-cut running shoes
- Mid-cut hiking boots for short trips with light loads
- High-cut backpacking boots designed to carry loads and for off-trail trekking

To decide which suits you best, consider what terrain and conditions you will be traversing and how much hiking you will be doing. If you plan to do one- to four-hour hikes, low-cut hiking shoes are sufficient. Mid-cut and high-cut boots take up plenty of space and weight, and are usually necessary when doing long-distance trekking.

On long-term trips, I always travel with my sturdy mid-cut hiking boots that are great for all types of hikes and treks. I also carry a pair of lightweight, waterproof sandals ideal for rafting and kayaking.

Sleeping Bag
Sleeping bags are only necessary if you plan to camp at least eighty percent of the time. If you are going on a three-day camping safari during a four-month journey, you are better off renting one from the tour operator. Most sleeping bags are rated in terms of several elements. These are the four main ones:

- **Temperature:** Choose a bag rated for the coldest temperature you expect to encounter. Most bags are rated according to the upper and lower temperature limits at which they will keep you warm or cool before discomfort sets in.
- **Weight vs. size:** Strike a balance between keeping weight low and ensuring comfort. It is wise to pick one that is moderately sized and can still provide sufficient comfort for a good night's sleep.
- **Type of insulation:** The two main types of fill in the market are down and synthetic. Down fill is light, compressible, breathable, and durable, although it is more expensive. DriDown® is down fill that is treated to resist moisture – a great insulation to look out for. Synthetic fill excels in wet and cold conditions, but is heavier and less compressible. Thanks to technology, new synthetic materials such as Thermolite® are designed for exceptional warmth, without the bulk.
- **Shape and fit:** Choose a mummy bag with narrower shoulder/hip ratio that maximizes thermal efficiency and carries less weight. Some people find it more restrictive and uncomfortable, but I find it keeps me snug and warm. Rectangular sleeping bags are less expensive and have plenty of space for your feet and head, but this becomes a negative feature in the cold.

Equipped with my trusty hiking boots and parka while hiking in Cradle Mountain National Park, Tasmania.

Packing Suggestions

You can travel farther and be happier if you carry less gear. The secret is to give up a few creature comforts in order to reduce the weight of your pack, without sacrificing anything you need or compromising your safety.

- Choose lightweight, quick-dry clothing such as drawstring trousers instead of heavy jeans.
- Pack layers of clothing when traveling in a cold climate, as it is the best way to protect yourself from the cold and it allows you to pack light.
- Bring a sarong – it's extremely versatile and can be used as a sleeping sheet, skirt, or beach towel.
- Use trekking sticks as tent poles, and a spork (combination of spoon and fork), when camping.
- To save space, either carry one book at a time or an e-book reader.
- Store documents such as boarding passes in your smartphone or other electronic device instead of carrying papers.
- Bring toiletries in small containers; you can always replenish them on the road.

Recommended Packing List for a Two-Week Trip
Keep in mind that you won't need much more than this for a month-long trip.

Useful items:

- Universal adapter
- Packing cubes to compartmentalize items
- Padlock to lock up backpack
- Headlamp
- Toiletries in small bottles
- Sunscreen
- Sunglasses
- Pocket knife
- Binoculars

Medication in a first-aid kit:

- Ibuprofen/Paracetamol
- Diarrhea pills
- Motion-sickness pills
- Antiseptic
- Antihistamine for allergies
- Insect repellent
- Oral rehydration pills
- Sanitary napkins and tampons

Clothing:

- Technical parka for cold weather
- Light waterproof jacket
- Long quick-dry pants
- Shorts
- Sarong for the beach
- Long-sleeved shirt
- Singlet/t-shirts
- Swimsuit
- Socks, bra and underwear
- Two pairs of footwear
- Wide-brimmed hat
- Sunglasses
- Quick-dry travel towel

Packing all my camping essentials into one kayak — Lysekil, Sweden.

A Step-by-Step Guide to Packing

1. Consider the weather during your visit.

2. Check the baggage weight limit for your flight.

3. Follow carry-on luggage rules according to your airline, some only allow as little as seven kilograms. If you plan to carry bottled liquid in your carry-on, make sure it is less than 100ml.

4. Pack all your electronics and delicate items in your carry-on bag instead of your check-in bag to make sure they stay safe.

5. Pack heavy items close to your spine. This ensures the weight of the pack is evenly distributed, and you will be comfortable carrying it for a longer time.

6. Consider which items you will need most regularly (such as toiletries, guidebook, and walking sticks), and place these on the external pockets for easy access.

7. Wear bulky items such as hiking boots and jeans on the plane instead of packing them.

8. Do not leave your packing until the last minute. Start a few days before departure. You will most likely have to cut down on your load. Do a trial run to make sure you can withstand the weight for a period of time.

Physical and Mental Training

Preparing yourself mentally and physically is important to ensure your safety and performance as you travel. Even if you do not plan any strenuous activities, bracing yourself helps put you in the right frame of mind.

Start by assessing the level of physical fitness required for the type of trip you have chosen. Check with your tour operator, research on travel blogs, or approach travelers who have done similar trips.

Examine your own fitness level and find out what you need to do to reach your goal. Ask yourself these questions: How often do you exercise? Have you done anything similar to this trip? Are you a beginner or an amateur in the sport?

For example, a one-week hiking trip in Jordan can be easily managed if you exercise regularly. A fifteen-day trek to the Mount Everest Base Camp, on the other hand, will require you to train specifically for the long trek, and get your lungs ready for the high altitude. If it is your first time traveling to high altitudes, it is wise to consult the altitude center to determine your body's sensitivity to low oxygen. These centers often conduct hypoxic training sessions where you will have the opportunity to exercise in oxygen-reduced air.

How to prepare for an active trip:

- Hit the gym at least three times a week. Focus on cardiovascular training for long treks.
- Walk long distances on consecutive days. Long periods of activity will help your body gain endurance.
- Eat a healthy, balanced diet; avoid fast food, and carbohydrate-based foods such as rice and bread.
- Spend your weekends hiking or camping in the countryside — camping in Africa for a month can be tough if you've never camped before.
- Test out your gear at home to make sure it works and that you know how to use it all.

- Take dietary supplements such as vitamins to make up for the minerals you may miss out on during the trip (especially for long camping trips and treks).

In some cases, you will require more mental training than physical:

- Even while lying in bed, visualize yourself reaching the top of a long hike in Nepal, or bungee jumping down a canyon in New Zealand.
- Do as much research as you can to visualize your task. Read about other people's experiences online and ask questions.

Climbing the rock pinnacles at Tsingy de Bemahara, Madagascar requires some physical effort.

> *I developed my own ways of dealing with the thought of remaining miles, and mainly they involved never seriously considering the distance ahead. I'd break it down into days; reaching the next tree, small sprints to a landmark, incentivizing myself with small rewards like a cold drink in a petrol station or a new view around a bend; or a free coast down the hill whose brow once seemed so far off. Adventure is about the reward of newness and finding personal development in experience earned the hard way.*

Dave Cornthwaite
Adventurer and author of Life in the Slow Lane;
davecornthwaite.com

On the Top of the World at Everest Base Camp

Solo female traveler Rebecca Enright, publisher of Backpacker Becki (backpackerbecki.com), shares her grueling experience of trekking to Mount Everest Base Camp.

I remember seeing the Everest Base Camp trek a few years ago, a random find that immediately made it onto my travel 'to do' list. Not only was Nepal high on my list of places to visit, but completing this would also be a fantastic achievement.

I had been that typical asthmatic kid at school, the one who was told I did not have to partake in strenuous athletic endeavors because it was obvious I was never going to make it and any attempt would just result in embarrassment. So I went through life not taking much interest in sport, or thinking I could not do much in the way of extreme physical exertion. It took me many years to realize that this is not the case, and Everest Base Camp was one of those things I had to do to prove that to myself.

In all honesty, I did not know what to expect from this epic trek. I knew it was going to be hard, but I never realized how hard. The most I had managed before this was a three-day jungle hike in Northern Thailand, which now feels like a walk in the park by comparison.

Leaving from Kathmandu, Nepal's capital, we braved an early-morning flight to the small town of Lukla on board a small, rickety aircraft. The engine roared for the full 40 minutes before touching down on a short, steep, and precarious mountainside runway.

Cheering at the successful landing, we went to breakfast full of excitement about the trek ahead – a three-hour uphill climb which was not too taxing. Little did we know how much harder it would be and how much colder it would get.

On day two, we made our way to Namche Bazaar, one of the biggest rest areas packed full of markets, restaurants, and cafes; reaching this town at 11,280 feet required extreme effort. It involved six hours of steep climbing through stunning forest, crossing rivers via vertiginous, swaying suspension bridges, and relentless physical exertion in the dusty, dry heat.

It was around days four and five that we started to feel the changes in the air. Just when we thought we had gotten our breath back, we were off again to reach a higher altitude, a dry-run ready to make the proper ascent the next day. We climbed high and slept lower, a painful but necessary evil that made the next trekking days a little easier.

A six o'clock wake-up call marked the start of the last day of our trek. By this point, each day had begun to feel like a relentless and monotonous struggle – except this was the day that we all hoped to find enough energy to pull through the last leg of our ascent to Everest Base Camp.

I didn't feel giddy with excitement that morning. Instead, swathed in five layers of clothing and still suffering after a severe cough and altitude headaches, I felt relieved that what I had set out to achieve was just a few hours away.

Over the course of six hours, we pulled ourselves slowly and sluggishly through the thin and icy air. Even the strongest of people were flagging. I remember one of the Sherpas grabbing my arm to hold me up, pulling me over rocks as my legs were about to give way and pushing me to the end. He refused to let me be defeated, especially not now that we had got this far.

When we reached the top of the final climb, stumbling over loose rocks and onto a canvas of white, all I could do was cry at what had become one of my greatest achievements – the top of the world was standing right before me. There wasn't a camp, or a huge sign signaling our end goal, but it didn't matter. I knew I had finished what I had set out to do.

Rebecca Enright reaches the Everest Base Camp and celebrates the greatest achievement of her life.

Protecting Your Health

Vaccination and Prevention
Consulting your doctor is the best way to find out which vaccinations you should get, depending on your destination. In some countries, it is mandatory to have certain vaccines before visiting. Be sure to start early, as some vaccines, such as Hepatitis A or B, require multiple shots over a three to six-month period.

A great resource is the Centers for Disease Control and Prevention website (cdc.gov), which lists regional diseases, risks, and health concerns for many countries around the world. The World Health Organization website (who.int) also offers a wealth of information.

Commonly recommended vaccinations include:

- Hepatitis A
- Hepatitis B
- Typhoid
- Yellow fever
- BCG (Tuberculosis)
- Tetanus
- Meningitis

Identifying Medical Problems
Regardless of where you are going, it is wise to educate yourself on the possible medical issues you may encounter. Taking good care of your health can be a difficult task in some developing countries due to the lack of infrastructure and medical supplies, so your best plan is to engage in risk-protection strategies. Always refer to a healthcare professional for correct preventive measures and treatments.

Dengue Fever

This disease is transmitted by day-biting mosquitoes, and is a major problem in many parts of Latin America and Southeast Asia (cases have also been reported in Samoa and Guam). As many as 100 million people are infected yearly.[2]

The symptoms are fever, headache, and severe joint and muscle pains. It can sometimes develop into dengue hemorrhagic fever, which is a severe form that is extremely rare in travelers.

There is no specific treatment or vaccination for dengue, although consulting a doctor or visiting the hospital is the recommended course of action. Do not take painkillers as they increase the risk of hemorrhaging. The best prevention is avoiding mosquito bites.

To avoid getting bitten, it is wise to cover yourself with long-sleeved shirts and trousers, especially at night. Try to sleep in a screened room, preferably under a treated mosquito net. Remember to spray your room with an insect spray every night before going to bed.

Malaria

Malaria is a serious and sometimes fatal disease caused by a parasite that commonly infects a certain type of mosquito that feeds on humans. It is a major risk in most parts of sub-Saharan Africa and South Asia. The Centers for Disease Control and Prevention has a malaria map that shows areas at risk.

Some symptoms include fever, chills and sweating, headache, diarrhea, abdominal pains, or simply a non-specific vague feeling of ill health. Without treatment it can rapidly become very serious, even fatal. Globally, the World Health Organization estimates that 219 million clinical cases of malaria occurred in 2010, with 660,000 deaths, most of them children in Africa.[3]

Taking anti-malarial pills is quite common, though their side effects can be an issue for some travelers. Most malaria pills are required to be started before departure to reach maximum protective levels by the time you arrive at your destination. Some common preventive medications include atovauone/proguanil (Malarone), chloroquine, and doxycycline. Refer to your doctor for usage and side effects.

You can buy anti-malarial treatments in most destinations, but beware of fake and substandard drugs. Always buy from a reputable pharmacy, perhaps one associated with a hospital or recommended by your embassy.

Considerations when choosing a drug for malaria:
- Recommendations for malaria-preventive drugs differ by country of travel and can be found in the country-specific tables at cdc.gov.
- No antimalarial drug is 100% effective, and all must be combined with preventative measures to avoid being bitten.
- For all medicines, also check online for the possibility of negative interactions with other medicines that you are taking (refer to the 'Resources' section).

Altitude Sickness

If you are planning on trekking or traveling in any high-mountain region (over 8,000 feet), you need to consider the risk of acute mountain sickness (AMS). Flying into high-altitude cities such as Cusco, Peru, may also leave you vulnerable to AMS. Physically fit individuals are not immune — even Olympic athletes get altitude sickness.

Symptoms of mild altitude sickness include headache, nausea, loss of appetite, shortness of breath, difficulty sleeping, and lack of energy. These are quite common when you first arrive at high altitude. The golden rule is to never continue to ascend if you have any symptoms of AMS. If the symptoms persist or worsen, you must descend. Get more information on AMS from a travel clinic or your expedition organizer.

Tips to Prevent Acute Mountain Sickness:

- Do a mountaineering consultation and altitude training at a travel clinic.

- Avoid flying to high altitude; start below 9,000 feet or travel overland.

- Always ascend slowly; you can climb more than 1,000 feet in a day as long as you come back down and sleep at a lower altitude.

- Chewing on coca leaves or drinking coca tea is a common preventative measure in South America.

- Stay hydrated. Acclimatization often results in fluid loss, so you need to drink at least four to six liters a day to keep yourself hydrated.

- Avoid tobacco, alcohol, and other depressants that may decrease the respiratory drive.

- Eat a high-calorie diet while at high altitudes.

- Consult your doctor before the trip for further advice.

High altitudes at Bolivia's Salar de Uyuni can leave you vulnerable to AMS.

Building a Safety Net with Activity Travel Insurance

Many travelers dismiss travel insurance as an unnecessary expense and waste of money. They couldn't be more wrong. Insurance is not a luxury item, it is essential, especially for adventure travelers who engage in risky activities or visit off-the-grid destinations. The process of finding the right policy may require time and effort, but it is definitely time well invested.

Keep in mind that most travel insurance policies do not cover outdoor activities such as biking, trekking, horse riding, or sailing. It is therefore crucial to find an activity insurance that will cover not only general travel-related incidents, but also the activities you will be participating in on the trip. Ask the tour operator you are traveling with if they offer travel insurance; some of them offer policies that automatically cover all activities undertaken on your trip.

If you travel more than three times a year, or are traveling for an extended period of time, you can save money by purchasing an annual travel insurance package to cover all your trips on one policy.

One of the most highly recommended policies is the Adventure Travel Protection Plan from Travel Guard, which covers trekking at high altitudes. The basic plan has coverage for trip cancellation, reimbursement for lost baggage and gear, and up to $500,000 for emergency evacuation.

When buying activity insurance, make sure you are entitled to these services:

- Medical treatment, hospital transportation, and repatriation if you fall ill or injure yourself.
- Monetary compensation for trip cancellation in the event of an emergency.
- Coverage for loss or theft of valuables, documents, money, and baggage, and repatriation of remains in the case of fatal incidents.

Tips on Buying Travel Insurance:

- Check if the policy covers your destination.
- Ask if the policy covers your interest (be it biking or trekking) as a primary activity. Many travel policies only cover cycling as an incidental activity, not a primary one.
- Find out what the excess of the policy is. This is the amount of money you need to pay for each claim. It may be worthwhile paying a higher premium for a policy with smaller excesses.
- Check the coverage limits. Most policies have a ceiling on the value of items to be insured, especially big-ticket items like cameras and laptops.
- Find out what documentation you need to supply to file a claim.
- Be honest about any pre-existing medical conditions you may have. Lying about your health conditions may give the insurance company the right to deny your claim.
- Some credit card companies provide limited travel insurance if you purchase your flight with their card. Ask your credit card company what it covers.
- Find out if the insurance company will provide any medical or emergency assistance on the road and if so, what information you will need when seeking assistance.
- Find out if you can renew the policy while on the road.
- Always check the fine print so you will be aware of every exclusion clause the policy may have.

ON THE ROAD

"It still holds true that man is most uniquely human when he turns obstacles into opportunities."

Eric Hoffer

Where Fear Meets Faith: Finding Courage in Life

Travel writer and sketch artist Candace Rardon (candacerardon.com) shares the experience that gave her courage in life.

For days, I had been having the same dream: each night found me in a small pod suspended by cables over a river gorge, bungee cord wrapped around my ankles. Each night, jumpers walked up to the ledge, screaming as they looked down. Attendants stood behind them, holding their shoulders and saying, "Conquer your fears. You have to jump."

Each night, I would wake up before my chance to jump ever came, just like in that dream where you fall but never hit the ground. Eternal suspension without resolution.

I was halfway through a year-long working holiday in New Zealand before I decided to take the plunge – a plunge better known as the Nevis Highwire Bungy. Measuring 439 feet, it is the highest bungee in the country, and the third highest jumping platform in the world. The commercial bungee jump was invented in New Zealand; jumping here is the equivalent of eating pizza in Italy or drinking champagne in France. You are at the source.

My decision to move to New Zealand had not been an easy one. Truth be told, I'd made it as a way to prove my feelings to a Kiwi I'd fallen for in London, but in the time between my decision and my departure, he let me know that we were just friends. Despite the heartbreak and humiliation, I decided to go anyway, my stubborn pride unable to back down from the move.

But on the day of my flight to Auckland, fear racked my mind. What if I couldn't find a job? What if I ran out of money? What if I failed?

As it usually does, reality proved more favorable than the worst-case scenarios my imagination had conjured up. I found jobs in Christchurch and Queenstown, got roommates, and made friends. I signed up for adventures – such as hiking the Franz Josef Glacier – but none that involved hurling myself into a great abyss.

At the jump site on a cloudless October morning, we signed safety waivers, donned harnesses, and weighed ourselves to determine the group's jump order. Finally, we boarded a gondola that conveyed us to the pod, where we trembled like lambs being led to the slaughter.

Three turns away from my jump, an attendant sat me up on a counter and tightened the straps around my calves. A friend looked over and asked, "Why are you so pale?"

One turn away, I was ushered into a seat that resembled a dentist's chair far too much for my liking. Another attendant began attaching a weight and clipping what felt like a hundred carabineers and ropes to my legs, all the while asking, "So this is your first time? How are you feeling?"

After a quick smile for the company's camera, it was go-time. Legs bound together, I waddled my way to the wooden jumping platform. As soon as he saw I was in position, a final attendant started counting.

"Three…"

Like a sailor dropping anchor at sea, he threw the weight over the ledge, which caused me to lurch forward ever so slightly.

"Two…"

There was no time to ask myself if I was ready. It was only, "Jump out, jump out, jump out." As much as I tried not to look down, I had to watch my feet as they inched nearer and nearer to the edge of the platform. Photos would later betray my complete hesitance, my shaky knees, and arms that refused to fully extend.

"One."

With a gentle nudge from the attendant, I pushed off – a scream escaping before I'd even left the platform. But almost instantly, something extraordinary happened. Something called freefall.

It would take eight and a half seconds for the cord attaching me to the pod to pull taut, and in that interval which seemed both impossibly short and strangely long, a sense of weightlessness overcame me, literally taking my breath away. I was falling, floating, flowing back to earth.

In two seconds, all my panic melted into peace, my fear into faith. Hours of dread gave way to those eight and a half seconds of resting in my trust that the cord would support me. What better metaphor for my decision to come to New Zealand, and for life itself.

Overcoming Your Fear

For many people, fear is the biggest obstacle to achieving personal goals. We give fear so much power that we sacrifice our dreams to avoid anxiety or the possibility of rejection or failure.

The first step towards dealing with fear is to recognize that it is inevitable. We all experience fear, whether first-time travelers or experienced adventurers. It is important to know that while it cannot be completely eliminated, fear can be managed. By facing fear with a clear and objective mind, you will realize that it is possible to fight it, focus on what you're doing, and achieve what you want in life.

Next, we need to realize that fear builds character, and teaches us how to act with courage. In a study on fear associated with extreme sports, conducted by Eric Brymer and Robert Schweitzer, a mountain climber described dealing with fear as 'empowering' and 'feeling very at peace', while a BASE jumper termed the pursuit as 'the ultimate metaphor for jumping into life rather than standing on the edge quivering.'[4] Confronting fear can be transformative, and equip us to deal with the tribulations of everyday life.

Start seeing fear as an opportunity — it can act as a guidepost to help us identify problems and solve them efficiently. When you feel afraid of something unfamiliar, take it as a sign that you need to get to know the place or situation better. If you are afraid of heights, think about the opportunities that will open up to you once you overcome it. Be motivated by the prospect of expanding your horizons to a different dimension.

By preparing in advance with proper information on risks and safety procedures, by training physically and mentally, and by assessing our skills and experience levels in relation to the adventure, it is possible to gain confidence and keep fear under control. It may take a huge leap of faith and a dollop of courage, but the results, and the journey along the way, are always well worth it.

> *In my line of work, skydiving, fear is what keeps you from getting careless. A healthy amount of apprehension has helped me to stay safe over a 20-year career. I am cautious enough to plan each one of my jumps carefully and to reject ideas when the risks were unacceptably high. Fear gets problematic when it becomes your focal point, dominating your thoughts and distracting you from the task at hand.[5]*

Felix Baumgartner
Extreme athlete who skydived from space during the October 2012 Red Bull Stratos jump

Paragliding can be a great way to overcome a fear of heights— Cape Town, South Africa.

Managing Your Fear in 5 Easy Steps

1. Visualize the results and the journey to get there. Make mental snapshots of the outcome and how you'll achieve it, and then set out to make it a reality. Each time fear creeps in, replace it with an image of success.

2. Break the cycle of negative thoughts. Think about something totally unrelated to the mission at hand and then come back to see the situation more objectively. Remember: you have the power to control your thoughts.

3. Don't let the momentum subside. It takes a certain amount of momentum to deal with fear. When you're faced with setbacks it can be tempting to give up. Stay determined and persevere, even when it seems impossible to reach your goal.

4. Make short-term goals. To make the task feel less intimidating, set smaller goals at intervals. Let's say you're doing a long trek; aim to walk to the next tree each day and then expand upon it as you get closer to your final goal.

5. Celebrate your victories. Give yourself a pat on the back for each milestone. When you see how good it feels to gain an edge on your fear, you'll be ready to face the next one head-on.

The Dangers and Rewards of Traveling to Forbidden Lands

In my years of traveling around the world, I have visited several places that are considered 'dangerous' by many, including North Korea, Burma (or Myanmar), the Palestinian Territories and Zimbabwe.

As a curious traveler, I believe seeing a place is the best way to dispel the myths surrounding them. Traveling is my way of gaining on-the-ground knowledge, and visiting these forbidden lands is how I get to know the country beyond the headlines.

My travel experiences have shown me that the reality of life in these places is often very different than what appears on the evening news, and that no matter what happens between governments, people are generally good.

Tourism can be a powerful tool to fight discrimination and advocate for equality. A profitable tourism industry not only helps to improve a country's economy but also bring peace. Egypt, for instance, needs tourists now more than ever to revive its tourism industry and an economy that suffered severely due to the revolution. South Sudan is a good example of a brand new country whose fragile economy could benefit substantially from visitors and tourism dollars.

With some safety precautions and advance planning, visiting these 'danger zones' can lead to gratifying travel experiences. There are, however, several things to keep in mind when traveling to these areas:

- Check blogs, websites, and forums to find out which parts of the destination are safe to visit.
- Follow the news to keep yourself updated on the political situation.
- Keep your plans flexible, and be open to last-minute changes.
- Register with your embassy before going. If caught in a dire situation, report to your embassy at the destination as soon as possible.

- Inform your family of where you'll be visiting and your hotel information. Leave instructions on who to contact if they don't hear from you after a certain period of time.
- When in the country, blend in by dressing conservatively and according to local custom, so as not to attract too much attention.
- Be respectful of the locals and their ideas and do not try to force your opinions on them.

Travel Advisories: Reliable or Exaggerated?

At the time of printing, the United States government had issued travel warnings against 35 countries where the American government's ability to assist their citizens is constrained. The United Kingdom's Foreign and Consular Office (FCO) also has a list of countries they advise citizens to avoid. Keep in mind that, in most cases, it is not the whole country that is off-limits but, rather, a specific area.

Reading the US Department of State's information on Belize, for example, might conjure up images of a country plagued by violent crimes such as armed robbery, gang warfare, and kidnapping. In my experience, the reality cannot be further from the truth. While crime exists in Belize City, like anywhere else, the islands are very safe and equipped with good tourism infrastructure. I would advise checking your country's travel advisory office before heading out, but supplement its advice with additional information from locals or travelers on the ground to get a more complete view of the actual situation at your destination.

Where to find foreign offices:

United States: The U.S. Department of State (travel.state.gov)
United Kingdom: UK Foreign and Commonwealth Office (fco.gov.uk)
Canada: Foreign Affairs, Trade and Development Canada (travel.gc.ca)
Australia: Australian Government Department of Foreign Affairs and Trade (smartraveller.gov.au)
New Zealand: New Zealand Ministry of Foreign Affairs & Trade (safetravel.govt.nz)

Only by visiting the wall that divides Israel and the Palestinian Territories did I understand the magnitude of the problem that the two nations face.

Seeing Past the Headlines in North Korea

At the shiny and ultra-modern Beijing airport, we boarded the Air Koryo Ilyushin Il-62 that would take us to Pyongyang, the capital of the Democratic People's Republic of Korea (DPRK), also known as North Korea.

Swathed in moss green upholstery and burgundy leather, the interior of the plane was reminiscent of the 1960's. Patriotic music played over the speakers as the immaculately dressed flight attendants served North Korean soft drinks and beers, and little platters of beans and pickles. Around us were mostly North Korean businessmen, dressed in white shirts and gray trousers, with small badges on their chests bearing portraits of their Supreme Leaders, Kim Il-Sung and Kim Jong-Il.

Landing in the 1950's-style concrete slab of an airport, my husband Alberto and I nervously got in line to pass through immigration. Customs officials clad in khaki army uniforms and communist-style caps examined our backpacks, pulling out our electronics and scrutinizing them with puzzled looks on their faces. We handed over our mobile phones – which would be retained in the airport during our visit – and passed through the swirling doors out of the terminal.

We were officially in the Hermit Kingdom, one of the world's terra incognita.

Since its separation from South Korea in 1948 after World War II, DPRK closed its doors to the outside world and retreated further and further into secrecy. Today, North Korea remains the least understood and longest standing Stalinist dictatorship in the world. Only 2,500 tourists visit each year (not including the Chinese who have good diplomatic ties). Foreign television, books, and the Internet are all forbidden.

So little of North Korea is known to the outside world that I did not know what to expect. I knew its strict tourism laws would require that we be herded from place to place, and shown only certain aspects of the country. At the same time, I knew it was an excellent opportunity to step away from the version of North Korea fed to us by the news media, and make my own judgment.

I didn't travel to North Korea to seek out the truth about its politics or government; I went to learn about the country from a humanistic point of view. To do so, I wanted to meet and interact with real people.

North Koreans are often portrayed by the outside world as humorless and robotic, but this stereotype was instantly broken once we met some residents. Riding on the subway, we were aware that locals were barely making eye contact with us, but one day, I noticed the lady sitting beside me was peeking at my camera screen as I scrolled through my photos. I leaned over and showed them to her, gesturing along the way in an attempt to communicate with her. She and her friends slowly warmed up to us, with fits of subdued laughter once in a while. We couldn't speak each other's language, but our gestures and body language formed a connecting bridge.

At Mount Ryonggak, we were enjoying an outdoor barbecue lunch when a big group of school children crowded around, watching us with curiosity. We smiled and waved. Most of them giggled coyly, while some bravely returned our greetings. I started asking their names and ages, but they couldn't understand me. An idea came to mind when I saw a few girls playing Rock, Paper, Scissors; I decided to use games to connect with them, rather than language. A whole series of charades and guessing games ensued. That lunch ended with gales of laughter, and possibly the best memories from the trip.

As we continued our walk towards the hilltop temple, we stumbled upon a party of North Korean ladies, playing drums and dancing in the woods. The gregarious bunch invited us to join in; with our spirits high, we were soon swaying our hands in the air and prancing around with these red-cheeked Korean housewives. The atmosphere was fun and relaxed, we felt as though this could be a Saturday anywhere else. This was not the North Korea that most people would imagine.

En route back to the car park, we fell into conversation with a band of soccer boys who had just finished a match. With our guides helping us to translate, we asked them about soccer and what they liked about the sport. To our surprise, they were spouting names of famous soccer players from Ronaldo to Zidane. Just like teenage boys anywhere else in the world, they loved football and dreamed of playing it professionally someday.

Regardless of the nation's political situation, I found a country with a spirit of camaraderie and pride, and people who were, in essence, just like you and me.

Please note: Visiting North Korea does not indicate that I am supporting of or encouraging the regime.

Meeting local children at Mount Ryonggak gave us a chance to understand North Korea from a humanistic point of view.

Risk Management in the Outdoors

Adventure activities, whether at home or abroad, carry some form of risk to health and safety. For those traveling to remote locations, additional risks include the lack of quick emergency response, poor trauma care, and unexpected weather changes that can make rescue efforts more difficult. Each outdoor activity has its own hazards; take time to research and be informed of every possible incident that can occur. Learning about these risks and the accessibility of resources will help make your trip a fun and safe adventure.

These precautions apply to all types of activities you may engage in:

- See your doctor a few weeks before the trip to make sure your health and physical fitness match up to the level recommended for the outdoor sports.
- Never participate in extreme sports alone. Joining a group, or having a partner who can assist you, or go for help if you get injured, is crucial.
- Avoid participating in any sport or activity when experiencing pain or exhaustion. Remember your health is more important than your pride or the money you've spent.
- Pay attention to warnings about climatic changes such as upcoming storms or severe drops in temperature. These may affect the activity you're doing.
- Do not drink alcohol before or during outdoor activities. Drink water regularly to stay hydrated and take time to rest if overheated.
- Wear appropriate protective gear such as goggles, helmets, gloves, and padding, and make sure equipment is in good working order and used properly.
- Equip yourself with proper footwear that provides warmth and dryness, as well as ample ankle support, especially when hiking in rough terrain.
- Always warm up before engaging in any physical activity. Cold and inactive muscles, tendons, and ligaments are more susceptible to injury.
- Stay grounded. Do not get over-confident and throw caution to the wind.

Trekking

The most important part of mountain climbing safety is to know the mountain you are trekking on and to show it proper respect. That means finding out the best climbing routes to the top, and making sure the routes are within your abilities. Study maps, and talk to climbers who are familiar with the mountain. It is always best to climb or trek in a team. When trekking together, you should always be aware of your team members' positions, as you rely on each other for support and rescue in case of emergencies.

The most obvious hazard that springs to mind is the danger of falling. Rough surfaces of exposed rock make it easy to break bones. You must be continually aware of the environment around you, and make sure your estimates of the strength and stability of the rocks are accurate.

Remember to stay vigilant during your descent. After summiting a mountain or completing a trail, you tend to feel you've accomplished your mission. That is when your safety is in jeopardy. Making it to the summit in one piece is only half the challenge; the other half is getting back down.

Weather is also a great threat, especially on the upper reaches of a mountain. Cold, snowy climates may make it very difficult to see the area ahead of you, while the altitude makes it more difficult to breathe. You may get stuck by unexpected disasters such as snowstorms. Climbers must be sure to bring proper support and have a back-up plan, regardless of their level of experience.

Here is some more trekking-specific advice to ensure your safety:

- Never forget to pack spare clothing that offers protection against the cold and the rain.
- Always carry a first-aid kit.
- Plan for an early start to avoid the heat or sun in the afternoon.
- Go at a moderate and regular walking pace, include sufficient breaks, and do not worry about keeping up with other trekkers.
- Make sure you have a sufficient supply of fluids. The best drinks to keep you hydrated are water or natural juices. Bring foods that are rich in nutrients, such as whole grain bread, dried fruits, and nuts.
- Always have consideration for the weaker members of your party. Advise other hikers of any dangers and give first aid in the event of an emergency.

Cycling

In 2011, there were more than 677 cycling deaths reported in the United States.[6] Even though these numbers represent approximately two percent of the total number of people killed in traffic accidents, it is still a considerable number that you do not want to be a part of.

The main cause of death in cycling is road accidents, specifically collision with a motor vehicle. Each country has its own road rules, so be sure to familiarize yourself with them. In France, for example, it is a legal requirement for riders to wear yellow reflective vests when cycling after dark. Keep in mind that some countries may not strictly enforce cycling rules, so keep an extra eye on vehicles that may pose a potential hazard.

For those planning a global bike tour, you will either need to bring your own repair kit or be able to turn to your bike insurance company in the event of breakdowns. Make sure you are equipped with some basic repair skills before you set out. Whether you plan to ride with a company or on your own, here are some ways to avoid common road hazards:

- Before setting off on a cycling tour, make sure you are comfortable and confident on your bicycle, and you know how to react quickly in case of emergency.
- If you are bringing your own bike and gear, do a few test runs before the trip by going on day trips with a loaded bike.
- Riding safely in big groups requires a mature and positive frame of mind. Be respectful to other riders around you, and communicate with them when passing or slowing down.
- Maintain your personal space and avoid close proximity to other bikes or vehicles.
- Instead of swerving around potholes (which may affect other riders nearby), learn to lightly roll or hop over potholes by pulling up the handlebar while lifting your feet.
- Riding in the rain can be dangerous, especially in the first minutes as the oil residue from cars creates a slick film before it is washed away. Try to go slower and maneuver your bike with extra care to avoid skidding.

- Road kill is quite a common sight in places like Australia. To avoid it, look about 20 yards up the road, not five.

Cyclists weaving through the magnolia fields of Bled, Slovenia.

Scuba Diving

According to the 'Diver's Alert Network (DAN) 2010 Diving Fatalities Workshop Report', a diving fatality occurs in one out of every 211,864 dives.[7] This number may seem very low to most of us, but there are still risks that we should be aware of before we take the plunge.

You should always be truthful about any medical problems before beginning dive training, and be sure to review your dive certification's medical questionnaire periodically even after certification.

Poor buoyancy control is an issue with many divers, even though this should be addressed during the certification process. Before attempting to dive, make sure you are clear on how pressure change affects your buoyancy underwater and how to control it. Clarify this with your instructor, or get some hands-on practice in a shallow pool beforehand.

Rapid ascents often occur when divers are not confident. As a result, they panic and rocket to the surface. This can cause pulmonary barotrauma (lung over-expansion) or decompression sickness. Never attempt a dive if you are not prepared.

"A 'good' diver is not the person with the most gear, or the one who dives the deepest," says DAN Medic Eric Schinazi. "It's the one who can make a mature decision that they should not make a dive."[8]

These issues all boil down to inadequate training – to avoid that, it is best to constantly practice and keep yourself up-to-date with the guidelines. I try to dive at least once every three months to keep my diving skills fresh. To ensure safety, I also make sure to let my instructor know my level of experience (how many dives I've done and when I did the most recent dive), and have a good chat with him/her beforehand.

Here are some safe diving practices:
- Assess yourself and your goals. Are you mentally prepared to dive? Is the dive causing you stress? These answers will help you determine if you are ready to go underwater.
- If the last dive you did was a few years ago, sign up for a scuba diving refresher course before attempting to dive again.
- Dive only when you are healthy, and your ears and sinuses are clear. The most common diving injury is ear barotrauma, often caused by congestion.
- Check your equipment even if your dive instructor or assistants have set it up for you. Properly functioning equipment is crucial in scuba diving.
- Choose a buddy whose skills and training are similar to your own. In cases when you are diving solo and you are not familiar with your buddy, make sure to spend some time learning each other's experience level and diving style.

Kayaking or Canoeing

In contrast to the other sports, kayaking or canoeing does not require much training or certification. As a result, it is easy to become complacent and underestimate the potential dangers of the river or sea.

Basic safe paddling practices include:

- Always bring another person, regardless of your skill level. Ideally, the other person should be in his or her own boat, to be best able to help in an emergency situation.
- Avoid weather or water conditions that are beyond your skill level; do not challenge yourself with conditions you are not prepared for.
- Make sure you are a competent swimmer, with the ability to handle yourself underwater and in moving water.
- Plan your route in advance, and identify potential hazards such as difficult rapids or dams. Devise an emergency plan.
- Carry a supply of food and water that can sustain you for the trip, but don't overload the boat with more weight than it can accommodate.
- Never go boating under the influence of alcohol or drugs.
- Always wear a properly fitted life jacket. The American Canoe Association reports that in 85% of paddling fatalities, the individual was not wearing a life jacket.[9]
- Do not stand up in a canoe or kayak; weight shifts may cause it to capsize. This accounts for almost half of all paddling fatalities.
- Never paddle over a submerged dam, fallen tree, or other obstacles. Try to avoid them by landing, if possible.
- Learn re-entry techniques and know some basic self-rescue techniques – such as various rolls – to avoid falling out of your sea kayak. If you are tossed out of your kayak, you should know how to use a flotation device and a rescue sling (floating rope) to get yourself back into the cockpit.

In addition to basic paddling equipment, you will also need several emergency items when paddling independently:

- Lifejacket
- Spray skirt
- Bilge pump
- Towline
- Flashlight
- Flare gun
- Knife

Kayaking amidst icebergs and glaciers in the Arctic requires extra safety preparations.

Skiing or Snowboarding

Every year in the United States alone, an average of 40 people lose their lives on the slopes as a result of skiing and snowboarding accidents, according to statistics compiled by the U.S. National Ski Areas Association.[10]

The International Ski Federation (FIS) has a ten-point code of conduct that includes such things as the unspoken rule that the skier or snowboarder in front has priority.[11] Following these guidelines can help keep you safe.

Most snow-sports injuries occur as the direct result of an isolated fall when you lose control, often traveling too fast for the prevailing conditions and on a slope inappropriate to your ability level. Some are true accidents, while other falls are due to sheer recklessness. Being aware of your surroundings and having a cautious attitude will help ensure your safety as well as that of others on the slopes.

A snow avalanche can be a life-threatening source of danger especially for free riders and backcountry alpine skiers. It is wise for free riders to attend an avalanche safety course to ensure they are well informed on what to do in dangerous situations.

In addition to the FIS guidelines, here are some general safety tips for winter sports:

- Wear a helmet at all times and get a pair of good quality wrist guards when snowboarding.
- Adapt your speed to your personal ability and to the prevailing conditions of terrain, snow, and weather as well as to the density of traffic.
- Avoid veering off the pistes and always make sure you go with a companion.
- Learn how to recognize warning signs and dangerous terrains and wear an avalanche beacon at all times, even when skiing certain resorts' sidecountry terrain.

> *I've always been a thrill-seeker and am very attracted to like-minded adventurers. However, as I am growing closer to my 50th landmark birthday, I find myself clamming up a bit.*
>
> *But there's one thing that I will never stop doing: skydiving. It is still the biggest thrill I have ever encountered. The exhilaration of climbing into a small plane starts the journey. The door to the plane is wide open and you know that you just have to jump. The thrill stares you straight in the face, as there is nothing out there, just the sky.*
>
> *You are free, you are alive, and you are consumed with a release that nothing else in the world can offer.*

Molly Blaisdell
Travel journalist and radio correspondent; HerJourneyTo50.com

Winter Survival: How to Avoid an Avalanche

Iain Mallory trained in the British Army Physical Training Corps to become a winter mountain leader. These tips were originally published on his blog MalloryonTravel.com.

- Never travel in avalanche-prone areas alone.
- Ensure all transceivers are working and switched to send.
- Be aware of the conditions, and be prepared to change the planned route if the risk appears high.
- Maintain a sensible distance between individuals, minimizing the risk to one person at a time.
- Prior to crossing any slope, assess the risk factor by digging a small snow pit and testing the cohesion between layers.
- Cross the slope one at a time and, if necessary, protect with a rope, belaying from an anchor point.

If an avalanche happens:

- Attempt to escape to the sides or find a natural shelter such as a large boulder.
- Discard any loose gear such as ice axe or poles.
- Shout once, then close your mouth, cover your nose and attempt to 'swim' to the surface.
- The majority of fatalities are from asphyxiation, with the victim's own breath forming a death mask as it freezes. Try to create a breathing space by ascertaining which way is up. Dribble some spittle from your mouth – if it runs down your chin you are upright, if not, then attempt to dig in the opposite direction with your arms.

Staying Healthy While Traveling

Once on the road, getting sick can be a major damper on your mood and well-being. Maintaining personal hygiene and keeping healthy is the best way to avoid contracting any diseases or infections.

Avoiding Contaminated Food and Water

The list of illnesses that result from contaminated food is shocking: from dysentery to diarrhea and typhoid. Some people think that food-related diseases can be contracted only in less developed nations, but you can get sick from food anywhere. These are some preventive measures:

- When buying bottled water, always check the seal carefully and make sure it has not been tampered with.
- Disinfect water using purifying tablets or filter devices such as SteriPEN that use ultraviolet light to destroy bacteria.
- Choose clean eateries popular with locals.
- Raw and lightly cooked meat and seafood can be a source of parasites; make sure to order both well done when in doubt.
- Fruit and vegetables are difficult to clean thoroughly. Make sure to cook them, or peel and wash in uncontaminated water.
- Avoid unpasteurized milk. Powdered milk is usually fine.
- Heating kills germs. Hot food is always safer than food left out in the open.

Warding Off Wildlife Attacks

Whether it is a bear, lion, or crocodile, encountering wild animals is always a possibility when traveling in remote locations. During a camping safari in Botswana, I awoke in the middle of the night to have a jackal follow me back to my tent; thankfully, it ran off, with only my sandals and nothing else.

Get information about local animals (such as bear activity or lion population), and the laws regarding self-defense, from park rangers or destination guides/sites.

- In the case of a dog attack, feed the canine a removable piece of clothing or a purse to get its jaws off you.
- For sharks and crocodiles, the best method of deterrence is striking the animals' nose or eyes. Hitting sharks' gills is also a good strategy.
- For bears, it is useful to carry a bear spray or intensely hot pepper spray to scare them off. Keep it handy and not at the bottom of your knapsack.
- Never store food in your tent and always dispose of cooked food in appropriate containers.
- If a bear attacks, make as much as noise as you can or throw rocks. Wildlife experts do not recommend playing dead if a bear attack appears to be predatory.[12]

Even a seemingly relaxed lion should not be messed with — Victoria Falls Reserve, Zimbabwe.

Preventing Accidents and Injuries

Accidents are the main cause of death for travelers. Make sure to know the risk you are getting into, and take these measures to avoid them.

- Do not drink alcohol when driving, swimming, or doing any activity.
- Check wind and water conditions before you swim in the sea, and look out for currents. Never swim alone.
- Always wear your seatbelt regardless of what others say.
- When renting a car, check the credibility of the rental company. It is not worth sacrificing your safety to save some pennies.
- If you are driving a motorcycle or scooter, always wear a helmet.
- Avoid traveling at night, especially in places that may be dangerous.

Walking in the countryside is a great way to keep fit while traveling — Nazareth, Israel.

How to Keep Fit While on the Go

Jeremy Albelda is a fitness enthusiast and the creator of The World or Bust (theworldorbust.com). Here he shares tips on how to keep in shape while traveling.

- **Eat more frequent meals throughout the day.**

  Having five to six small meals throughout the course of the day will keep your metabolism revved up, providing you with sustained energy and no afternoon crashes. You will also burn a few extra calories just in the digestive process. Eating in this manner will let you sample more types of food while at your destination.

- **Do a physical activity twice per week.**

  Wherever I'm traveling, I like to check out the local gym culture, which I find interesting. If the gym isn't your thing, head to a local park, go hiking in the countryside or play soccer or Frisbee. You can also do push-ups, crunches, and arm curls with nothing more than a couple of water bottles. Try lifting your suitcase or bag for added resistance.

- **Walk, Walk, Walk!**

  One of the best ways to burn off excess calories is by walking. You'll get to see all the sights along the way, save money on transportation, and get some physical activity in.

- **Get your rest.**

  If you're traveling for months across time zones and borders, chances are you're going to be worn out getting from place to place. Do yourself a favor and make sure to sleep enough at night.

- **Limit how much alcohol you drink.**

  Going out at night while traveling offers a great way to meet new people; one issue with drinking too much alcohol is its high calorific content. The best thing to do is have a drink mixed with water or opt for a light beer instead, and – you guessed it – dance!

Responsible Travel Ethics

As travelers, it is our responsibility to ensure the activities we engage in protect the environment and support communities. When traveling with an operator, we need to look beyond the eco-friendly claims, and ask what they are really doing to support the environment, local people, animals, and plants.

Tread lightly with these general tips:

- **Leave no trace.** Do not leave garbage anywhere, or take anything from the environment. Stay on designated walking trails and camping spots, and always bring a trash bag to carry your waste with you. If there are no established toilets, relieve yourself at least 200 feet away from rivers and lakes.
- **Reduce your carbon footprint.** Offset your carbon emissions and reduce pollution by taking trains, ferries, or bicycles instead of flying.
- **Look for eco-friendly hotels.** Check if hotels have a written policy on their environmental efforts. Indicate to the hotel's cleaners that you don't need your towels and sheets changed daily. Switch off lights whenever you're not in the room, or open the windows instead of using the air conditioning.
- **Support local businesses.** Hire a local guide instead of a foreigner. Your money goes directly to the community, and locals tend to be more knowledgeable about the destination. Whenever possible, visit locally owned establishments, including guesthouses, restaurants, and shops.
- **Respect local culture.** Learn a few basic words in the local language; people always appreciate your interest in learning their culture. Simple words like "hello" and "thank you" can go a long way. Dressing appropriately in a conservative environment will allow you to fit in better.
- **Avoid aggressive bargaining.** While some vendors do expect you to bargain, remember that your purchases directly affect their livelihood. Decide if you want to hang on to that extra dollar or if it could help them more.
- **Reduce, reuse, and recycle.** Disposing of your garbage properly, and minimizing your electricity and water consumption, will benefit the overall destination. Reuse a bottle by refilling it from safe water sources or by disinfecting tap water with tablets.

"*We've been extremely fortunate to visit some of the world's most incredible destinations, from the Galapagos Islands and the Amazon to Patagonia and Antarctica. Exploring the world's most pristine ecosystems, seeing their endangered species, and understanding their indigenous cultures have enriched our lives immeasurably.*

But the sum benefits of ecotourism cannot be measured in the amount of wilderness preserved, species saved, or economic impact on developing nations. There are intangible benefits as well, changing us and altering the way we perceive our role in the universe. The more of these life-changing experiences we have, the more eager we become to protect these places from the ravages of climate change, unsustainable development, and exploitation."

Bret Love and Mary Gabbett
Co-Founders, GreenGlobalTravel.com and EcoAdventureMedia.com

When Tourism Goes Wrong

In Northern Vietnam, thousands of grottos and limestone cliffs dot the emerald waters of Ha Long Bay. Junk boats ply its water, against the natural backdrop of dark green rock formations shrouded in mist. As a UNESCO World Heritage Site, the attraction is easily the most visited site in the country.

Without proper regulations and safety standards in place, Ha Long Bay has unfortunately fallen victim to environmental issues and fatal accidents. In 2011, a boat sank, killing twelve tourists and shocking the world with the tragic news.[13]

Before our second trip to Vietnam, we found ourselves in a dilemma: visit Ha Long Bay and contribute to the existing environmental problems or skip it altogether but possibly miss one of the country's most beautiful sites. We had heard some travelers sing the praises of Ha Long Bay, while others ranted about the pollution and unethical behavior of local operators.

By the time we arrived in Hanoi, we were convinced we had to see it for ourselves. We booked an overnight boat trip on a mid-range vessel with few expectations, and a glimmer of hope that it would not disappoint.

Even before boarding our boat, we found a thick layer of oil and rubbish floating on the surface of the water just off the shore of the gateway town, Bãi Cháy. With poorly maintained facilities and a less-than-desirable build, our junk boat was nothing like the operator had promised.

In a fragile environment like Ha Long Bay, it is important to travel only with responsible tour operators – and in this situation, we had obviously made a mistake.

Upon sailing into the open waters, it was clear we were not going to be the only boat around. Ten others were sailing in the same direction. By the time we got to our first stop, we were in the company of twenty other boats and hundreds of people clambering up into the cave.

As we docked, a neighboring boat was cruising too close for comfort. We watched, amused and slightly horrified, as it sped past us, missing our boat by just a few inches. Our captain followed suit, squeezing his way between two other junks. The bow of the neighboring boat unfortunately hit one of our travel mates on the back. This time, no one was laughing.

Back in the cave, we walked elbow to elbow with at least a hundred other tourists and were dismayed to find soft drink cans and plastic bags strewn all over the place.

A massive construction project was underway by the cave, turning the emerald water a murky brown color. Our guide said they were building a port, to accommodate even more boats. I couldn't help but cringe: was this not enough already?

The next morning, we awoke to the sound of boats setting sail around us, and our engine blasting through the walls. Dropping anchor in a narrow bay, we hopped onto a floating village to get into our kayaks for the morning paddle. The smell of the contaminated water was unbearable, and the pollution even more so; dead fish and clusters of rubbish were floating on the oily water.

As we paddled out into the sea, we saw a junk boat sailing right into our travel mates, refusing to give way and almost running into them. Just last year, a pair of kayakers were hit by a boat, but fortunately survived the accident. Safety is apparently not a priority here.

By the end of the trip, we were more than ready to leave the bay. The beauty of the poetic landscapes was undeniable, but the sheer amount of environmental destruction was enough to put off any traveler with a conscience.

Following the accident, new regulations were introduced to tighten the operation of tourist boats. The Quang Ning People's Committee has set up new rules for the construction of tourist boats, including the elimination of wooden boats. New requirements call for at least two staff on board to have first-aid training, and boats to be equipped with standard fire-suppression systems.

I won't be returning to Ha Long Bay until the water is cleaned up and the situation controlled with new safety rules and measures. I can only hope the situation will improve and Vietnam will allow this natural wonder to regain its original beauty.

The beauty of Vietnam's Ha Long Bay is undeniable, but the irresponsible behavior of local tour operators is enough to put off any traveler with a conscience.

Handling Setbacks: What to Do When Something Goes Wrong

All travelers know that a trip with no glitches is a rarity. From common flight delays to severe emergencies, travel may bring with it some form of risk or hurdle. Here are a few of the most common setbacks, together with solutions that can help you in your hour of need:

Injuries
One of the biggest hazards for trekkers and skiers or snowboarders is falling. When an incident like this happens, calm yourself down and assess the situation logically before making any move. As it is with most activities that take place in the remote outdoors, things can change faster than you can react to them. If you are not the one injured, provide comfort to the victim and use basic first aid knowledge to reduce the victim's pain, if possible. Get help immediately via your phone or your nearest ranger station if you have no cell reception.

Road Accidents
In the event that you are injured in a road accident, seek medical assistance immediately using either your phone or help from people nearby. Take down all the details of the other people involved in the accident and speak to your insurer as soon as possible. It is useful to learn the basic legal rules of liability to find out who is responsible for an accident. Cyclists who don't follow road rules or don't keep a proper lookout might be deemed responsible for an accident.

Vehicle Breakdowns
It is important when driving in a foreign country to be prepared for your vehicle to fail. It can be dangerous if you are stranded without food and water, so make sure you pack plenty of snacks, drinks, and blankets, just in case. Many car rental companies will include breakdown coverage in the cost of your hire. For immediate assistance, seek help from the nearest town or village. Most people are more than willing to help.

Flight Delays

If your flight is delayed, it is important to know your rights to figure out what you are entitled to. When your flight to or from a European Union (EU) country on an EU-registered airline is delayed by more than two hours, EU regulations state you are entitled to meals, refreshments, and two free telephone calls or emails. If your flight is delayed overnight, you are entitled to hotel accommodation and transfers. There are no federal regulations about compensation following delays when flying within the US, but many US-based airlines do offer compensation to delayed passengers.

Baggage Delays and Loss

If your luggage does not appear on the carousel when you land, head straight to the baggage claim counter for your airline. If the airline claims that any missing baggage will arrive on the next flight, make sure that you get a firm assurance based on actual knowledge about your bag's location. You can make a legal claim for compensation if your baggage does not appear after 21 days. To find out how much compensation you are entitled to, check with your insurance provider.

Robbery/Theft

Dealing with being robbed while you are traveling can be difficult, but don't be afraid to go to the local police. You will need the police report for any claim you might later make through your travel insurer. Contact your bank immediately to have your credit cards canceled.

Illness

The advice to anyone who falls ill while traveling is to always immediately seek medical assistance. Get treatment from the nearest clinic or hospital if your symptoms worsen. If it looks as though your trip is going to be significantly disrupted by your illness, consider traveling home. Your travel insurance may cover the cost of your medical bills and even your flight home, so make sure you read the fine print.

If you are faced with a mountain, you have several options.

You can climb it and cross to the other side.

You can go around it.

You can dig under it.

You can fly over it.

You can blow it up.

You can ignore it and pretend it's not there.

You can turn around and go back the way you came.

Or you can stay on the mountain and make it your home.

–Vera Nazarian
The Perpetual Calendar of Inspiration

An Adventure Awaits

In the opening chapter of this book, I talked about adventure travel as a frame of mind, rather than as a type of travel. As I started researching this book and talking to other adventurers, it became clear to me that the greatest challenge that most people face is getting into this mindset. What is stopping them? Fear.

Through the subsequent chapters, I've shown you that with the right amount of preparation and safety precautions, it is possible to keep your fears at bay, and focus on what you really want to achieve.

In my personal process of writing this book, I ran into numerous obstacles that I had to overcome. By applying things I learned through travel to the book-writing process, I not only completed the mission at hand but I also thoroughly enjoyed every part of it.

Indeed, travel has given me all sorts of skills and knowledge that I have used to conquer many challenges in my life. Having jumped through hoops to attain my nomadic lifestyle, I have come to realize that I can overcome anything in life as long as I set my mind to it — and that is all thanks to travel.

You know that bungee jump I talked about at the beginning of the book? It changed my life forever. And believe me, it will change yours too.

A leap of faith — Khao Sok, Thailand.

Useful Websites

- Couchsurfing: couchsurfing.org
- Global Freeloaders: globalfreeloaders.com
- Servas: servas.org
- Hospitality Club: hospitalityclub.org
- Trusted House Sitters: trustedhousesitters.com
- HouseCarers: housecarers.com
- The Caretaker Gazette: caretaker.org
- Home Exchange: homexchange.com
- Love Home Swap: lovehomeswap.com
- Roof Swap: roofswap.com
- WWOOF: wwoof.net
- Grow Food: growfood.org
- Help Exchange: helpx.net
- Workaway: workaway.info
- Work Boat: workboat.com
- Crew Bay: crewbay.com
- All Yacht Jobs: allyachtjobs.com

Travel Insurance

- World Nomads: worldnomads.com
- Worldwide Insure: worldwideinsure.com
- Travel Guard: travelguard.com
- Mondial Assistance: mondial-assistance.com
- Ault Insurance Brokers for UK and European citizens: ault.co.uk
- IMG International Medical Group: imglobal.com
- Clements Worldwide for electronics/possessions: clements.com
- Handy insurance chart to compare plans: bootsnall.com/travelinsurance

Specialists in Activity Insurance

- Sports Cover for active holidays: sportscover.com
- Top Notch Cover can cover activities with extra premiums: topnotchcover.com
- Snowcard for UK residents: snowcard.co.uk
- Dive Assure for divers: diveassure.com
- A comparison chart for biking insurance: money.co.uk/bicycle-insurance

Visa Information

- For American citizens: travel.state.gov/travel/travel_1744.html
- For Canadian Citizens: voyage.gc.ca/index-eng.asp
- For UK Citizens: fco.gov.uk/en/travel-and-living-abroad/passports1/entryrequirements
- For Australian Citizens: dfat.gov.au/visas/index.html

Health Information

- Centers for Disease Control and Prevention: cdc.gov
- World Health Organization: who.int
- Masta: masta-travel-health.com
- Drugs.com for drug interactions: drugs.com/drug_interactions.php

Altitude Centers:

- London, United Kingdom: altitudecentre.com
- Sydney, Australia: sydneyaltitudetraining.com
- Gold Coast, Australia: altitudetrainingcentre.com.au
- Flagstaff, USA: hypo2sport.com
- Glendale, USA: infinityparkatglendale.com

Technical Planning Books

Trekking

- *Adventure Trekking: A Handbook for Independent Travelers,* by Robert Strauss
- *Backpacking: A Woman's Guide,* by Adrienne Hall
- *Beyond Backpacking: Ray Jardine's Guide to Lightweight Hiking,* by Ray Jardine
- *Day Hiker's Handbook: Getting Started with the Experts,* by Michael Lanza
- *Everyday Wisdom: 1001 Expert Tips for Hikers,* by Karen Berger
- *The Backpacker's Handbook,* by Chris Townsend
- *The Complete Walker IV,* by Colin Fletcher and Chip Rawlins
- *The Ultimate Hiker's Gear Guide,* by Andrew Skurka

Biking

- *Adventure Cycle-Touring Handbook,* by Stephen Lord
- *Bicycling Science,* by David Gordon Wilson
- *Essential Bicycle Maintenance & Repair,* by Daimeon Shanks
- *The Bicycling Guide to Complete Bicycle Maintenance & Repair,* by Todd Downs
- *The Complete Book of Long-Distance Cycling,* by Edmund R. Burke and Ed Pavelka
- *The Man Who Cycled the World,* by Mark Beaumont
- *Zinn & the Art of Road Bike Maintenance,* by Lennard Zinn

Scuba Diving

- *Dive Atlas of the World,* by Jack Jackson
- *Diver Down: Real-World Scuba Accidents and How to Avoid Them,* by Michael Ange
- *Dive in Style,* by Tim Simond
- *Dive Like a Pro: 101 Ways to Improve Your Scuba Skills and Safety,* by Robert N. Rossier

- *Neutral Buoyancy: Adventures in a Liquid World,* by Tim Ecott
- *PADI: Open Water Diver Manual,* by PADI
- *Silent World (National Geographic Adventure Classics),* by Jacques Cousteau
- *The Complete Diver: The History, Science and Practice of Scuba Diving,* by Alex Brylske
- *The Certified Diver's Handbook,* by Clay Coleman

Kayaking or Canoeing

- *Canoeing Basics,* by Melinda Allan and Ronald Carboni
- *Paddle Your Own Canoe: An Illustrated Guide to the Art of Canoeing,* by Gary McGuffin and Joanie McGuffin
- *Sea Kayaker Magazine's Handbook of Safety and Rescue,* by Doug Alderson
- *The Coastal Kayaker's Manual: The Complete Guide to Skills, Gear, and Sea Sense,* by Randel Washburne
- *The Basic Essentials Of Sea Kayaking,* by Mike Wyatt
- *The Complete Sea Kayaker's Handbook,* by Shelley Johnson

Skiing

- *Breakthrough on Skis I: Expert Skiing Simplified,* by Lito Tejada-Flores
- *Essential Guide: Snowboarding,* by Greg Goldman
- *Skiing and Snowboarding: 52 Brilliant Ideas for Fun on the Slopes,* by Cathy Struthers
- *Ski Mountaineering,* by Peter Cliff
- *Snowboarding the World (Footprint),* by Matt Barr, Chris Moran and Ewan Wallace
- *Snowboarding Skills: The Back-to-Back Basics Essentials for All Levels,* by Cindy Kleh
- *The ABC of Avalanche Safety,* by Ed Lachapelle
- *The Truth About Skiing and Snowboarding,* by Danko Puskaric

Books in The Traveler's Handbooks Series

- *The Career Break Traveler's Handbook*, by Jeff Jung
- *The Cruise Traveler's Handbook*, by Gary Bembridge
- *The Family Traveler's Handbook*, by Mara Gorman
- *The Food Traveler's Handbook*, by Jodi Ettenberg
- *The Luxury Traveler's Handbook*, by Sarah and Terry Lee
- *The Solo Traveler's Handbook*, by Janice Waugh
- *The Volunteer Traveler's Handbook*, by Shannon O'Donnell

Adventure Travel Blogs

- AlastairHumphreys.com
- CandaceRardon.com
- ExpertVagabond.com
- FamilyonBikes.org
- FourJandals.com
- InsidetheTravelLab.com
- Matt-Gibson.org
- OttsWorld.com
- ThePlanetD.com
- UncorneredMarket.com
- Vagabondish.com
- WanderingEarl.com
- WildJunket.com

Checklists

- Travel gear checklist: travelsmith.com/TravelSmith/US/TravelCenter/guide-packing-checklist/landing-path

- Mountain Equipment Co-op (MEC) trip checklists for various sports: mec.ca/AST/ContentPrimary/Learn/Watersports/TripChecklists.jsp
- Mountaineering gear checklist: backpacker.com/mountaineering_gear_checklist/gear/12101
- Bicycle touring gear checklist: bicycletouringpro.com/blog/jim-dirlams-complete-bicycle-touring-gear-checklist/
- Scuba equipment checklist: dutchsprings.com/PrintChecklist.pdf
- Kayaking gear checklist: seakayakermag.com/PDFs/Gearlist.pdf
- Backcountry skiing gear checklist: utemountaineer.com/Checklists/BackcountrySkiing.pdf

Endnotes

[1] Global catches, exploitation rates, and rebuilding options for sharks, wormlab.biology.dal.ca/pressmaterial/catches_exploitation/content/Worm_etal_EMBARGOED.pdf, (21 December, 2012).

[2] Centers for Disease Control and Prevention, cdc.gov/dengue, (26 June, 2013).

[3] World Health Organization, who.int/mediacentre/factsheets/fs094/en, (March, 2013).

[4] Christian Jarrett, "It's about accepting that you're mortal"- Extreme sports enthusiasts on overcoming fear, BPS Research Digest, bps-research-digest.blogspot.com.es/2013/05/its-about-accepting-that-youre-mortal.html, (8 May, 2013).

[5] Felix Baumgartner, How to Overcome Fear by Skydiver Felix Baumgartner, Bloomberg Business Week,businessweek.com/articles/2013-04-11/how-to-overcome-fear-by-skydiver-felix-baumgartner, (11 April, 2013).

[6] Bicycle Crash Facts, Bicyclinginfo.org, bicyclinginfo.org/facts/crash-facts.cfm, (2012).

[7] Divers Alert Network, diversalertnetwork.org/files/Fatalities_Proceedings.pdf, (2010).

[8] Divers Alert Network, DAN's Diving Tips for the New Diver, diversalertnetwork.org/medical/articles/DANs_Diving_Tips_for_the_New_Diver, (1997).

[9] American Canoe Association, Critical Judgement — Understanding and Preventing Canoe and Kayak Fatalities, c.ymcdn.com/sites/www.americancanoe.org/resource/resmgr/sei-educational_resources/critical_judgement_aca.pdf, (2003).

[10] Paul Gittings, edition.cnn.com/2013/01/14/sport/skiing-risks-deaths-injuries, CNN, (14 January, 2013).

[11] International Ski Federation, FIS General Rules, fis-ski.com/uk/insidefis/fisgeneralrules/10fisrules.html, (2002).

[12] Anahad O'Connor, The Claim: If Attacked by a Bear, Play Dead, New York Times, www.nytimes.com/2005/10/04/health/04real.html?_r=1&, (4 October, 2005)

[13] BBC News Asia-Pacific, bbc.co.uk/news/world-asia-pacific-12490523, (17 February, 2011).

The Adventure Traveler's Handbook

Nellie Huang

Nellie Huang is a professional travel writer and editor specializing in adventure travel and unusual experiences. In her quest for adventure, she has swum in the cold waters of Antarctica, trekked the jungles of Madagascar, skydived in Spain, and climbed an active volcano in Iceland, all of which she chronicles on her blog, WildJunket (wildjunket.com). She has been featured in BBC Travel, CNN, Huffington Post, Wend, and Women Adventure Magazine, amongst others. She is also a contributing guidebook author of VIVA Travel Guide Guatemala. When not traveling, she lives in Spain with her husband.

Nellie Huang

The Adventure Traveler's Handbook

Nellie Huang

www.ingramcontent.com/pod-product-compliance
Lightning Source LLC
Chambersburg PA
CBHW041218070526
44584CB00001B/6